Ruby Essentials
Mastering the Core Concepts and Practices

Adam Jones

Contents

Preface

Welcome to *Ruby Essentials: Mastering the Core Concepts and Practices*, a comprehensive guide aimed at equipping you with a deep understanding of Ruby's foundational principles and advanced practices. This book is crafted for learners who seek to grasp the core of Ruby programming—an elegant, expressive language known for its productivity and simplicity.

Ruby's design philosophy emphasizes the joy of programming, encapsulating the principle of least surprise. This book captures that essence, taking you on a journey from the fundamental building blocks to the advanced techniques that showcase Ruby's flexibility and power. Whether you are new to programming or an experienced developer wishing to hone your Ruby skills, this text will guide you in mastering the language's intricacies.

The structure of this book is methodically crafted to facilitate a progressive and holistic learning experience. We commence with an introduction to Ruby's rich ecosystem, accentuating its relevance in contemporary software development and its position among modern programming languages. This sets the stage for an in-depth exploration of Ruby's syntax, data structures, and core elements.

Successive chapters focus on the integral components of programming, including variables, data types, and control flow mechanisms. You'll learn how to harness these tools to construct effective scripts and applications. We then delve into Ruby's object-oriented paradigm, offering insights into class design, inheritance, and polymorphism, essential for building robust software projects.

Advanced topics such as exception handling, debugging strategies, and the utility of Ruby's powerful modules and mixins are meticulously explored, broadening your capabilities to navigate real-world challenges. Furthermore, we investigate File I/O operations and the manipulation of external libraries and gems, enabling you to enhance your applications with third-party solutions.

This book caters to a diverse audience. Novice programmers will find it a lucid introduction to the concepts underpinning Ruby and programming at large. Meanwhile, developers seasoned in other languages will discover a wealth of information regarding Ruby's unique features and idiomatic practices. Each chapter is designed to be a standalone resource, offering in-depth explanations and illustrative code examples that encapsulate best practices and innovative solutions.

By book's end, you'll possess a profound comprehension of Ruby's core concepts and practices, ready to craft your own sophisticated applications. This book is your gateway to becoming a masterful Ruby developer, whether you aim to embark on your programming journey or expand your existing toolkit with Ruby's nuanced capabilities. Let's begin this exploration into the art and science of Ruby programming, and uncover the elegance and potential the language holds.

Chapter 1

Introduction to Ruby and its Ecosystem

Ruby is a dynamic, open-source programming language with a focus on simplicity and productivity. It has an elegant syntax that is natural to read and easy to write. This chapter provides an overview of Ruby's origins and its underlying philosophy, discusses the Ruby ecosystem including version management tools, development environments, and RubyGems. Additionally, it touches upon the supportive Ruby community and outlines common coding conventions, setting the stage for a deeper exploration into the language.

1.1 The Birth of Ruby: Origin and Philosophy

Ruby, created by Yukihiro "Matz" Matsumoto in the mid-1990s, emerged from a desire to blend the best features of his favorite languages, namely Perl, Smalltalk, Eiffel, Ada, and Lisp. Matz aimed to form a new language that emphasized human needs over those of the computer, a philosophy that deeply influenced Ruby's development. This focus on human-centric design is encapsulated in the principle known as MINASWAN, an acronym for "Matz Is Nice And So We Are Nice," reflecting the welcoming and positive nature of the Ruby community.

The inception of Ruby was driven by Matz's dissatisfaction with existing programming languages. He sought to create a language that was truly object-oriented, easy to use, and more powerful than Perl, and yet more object-oriented than Python. Ruby's philosophy can be summarised by its two guiding principles: simplicity and productivity. The language's syntax is designed to be intuitive and straightforward, allowing programmers to express concepts in fewer lines of code without sacrificing readability. This design philosophy makes Ruby particularly well-suited for beginners, while still being powerful enough for complex software development tasks.

One of the fundamental concepts in Ruby is the principle of "least surprise," which means the language should behave in a way that minimizes confusion for experienced users. This principle guides the development of Ruby's features and APIs, ensuring that the language remains consistent and predictable. For example, when refinements were introduced in Ruby 2.0, they were designed to be scoped and explicit to avoid altering the behavior of existing code unpredictably, thus adhering to the principle of least surprise.

Ruby's philosophy is also evident in its approach to problem-solving. Ruby encourages flexibility and offers multiple ways to achieve a task, promoting creativity and exploration among developers. This flexibility is balanced with a strong emphasis on convention over configuration, a principle that suggests developers should follow standardized programming conventions unless they have a compelling reason to deviate. This balance between flexibility and convention supports a development culture that is both innovative and efficient.

Consider the following simple Ruby code example that demonstrates the language's natural syntax and emphasis on human readability.

```
1  def greet(name)
2    puts "Hello, #{name}!"
```

```
3   end
4
5   greet('World') # Output: Hello, World!
```

This example illustrates Ruby's clear syntax, where a method greet is defined to print a greeting. The string interpolation within #"", a feature borrowed from Perl but made simpler and more readable, showcases Ruby's emphasis on making code natural to read and write.

Given its emphasis on productivity and simplicity, Ruby has grown beyond its initial user base to become a favorite among web developers, particularly with the advent of the Ruby on Rails framework. The language's design, which balances flexibility with the principle of least surprise, continues to attract developers seeking a powerful yet user-friendly programming environment.

Ruby's journey from an idea in Matz's mind to a worldwide community illustrates the impact of its underlying philosophy. The language continues to evolve, but its commitment to simplicity, productivity, and catering to the needs of developers remains steadfast, ensuring Ruby's place in the landscape of programming languages for years to come.

1.2   Understanding the Ruby Ecosystem

The Ruby ecosystem comprises a myriad of components that collectively support the development, distribution, and execution of Ruby applications. Key among these components are the Ruby interpreter, a variety of development tools, an extensive collection of libraries (gems), package management systems, and a vibrant community that contributes to and maintains these assets.

The Ruby Interpreter

At the heart of the Ruby ecosystem is the Ruby interpreter. This is a program that executes Ruby scripts. Ruby's interpreter is designed to be simple yet powerful, emphasizing productivity and simplicity in programming. Unlike compiled languages where code must be transformed into machine-readable format before execution, Ruby code is interpreted line-by-line at runtime, making it easier to write and debug. The most commonly used Ruby interpreter is MRI (Matz's Ruby Interpreter), named after Yukihiro Matsumoto, the creator of Ruby.

Development Tools

Development tools in the Ruby ecosystem are designed to aid in the creation, testing, and maintenance of Ruby applications. These tools include Integrated Development Environments (IDEs) such as RubyMine and text editors like Sublime Text and Visual Studio Code with Ruby extensions. These environments provide syntax highlighting, code completion, debugging tools, and more to streamline the development process.

In addition to IDEs and text editors, other essential development tools include:

- `Rake` - a make-like task runner built in Ruby. It allows the definition of tasks and dependencies in Ruby.

- `RSpec` and `Minitest` - popular testing frameworks that facilitate behavior-driven development (BDD) and test-driven development (TDD).

- `RuboCop` - a static code analyzer and formatter that enforces many of the guidelines outlined in the community Ruby Style Guide.

Libraries and Gems

RubyGems, the package management system for Ruby, plays a critical role in the ecosystem by simplifying the process of discovering, installing, and publishing Ruby libraries (known as gems). Each gem contains a packaged Ruby application or library that can be easily distributed and integrated into other Ruby projects. RubyGems.org serves as the primary repository for these gems, hosting tens of thousands of packages covering a vast array of functionalities, from web frameworks like Rails to utilities for API consumption, data processing, and beyond.

To install a gem, the following command is used:

```
1   gem install <gem_name>
```

Upon execution, the specified gem and its dependencies are fetched from RubyGems.org and installed on the local machine. This simplicity in managing external libraries significantly accelerates development and encourages code reuse within the Ruby community.

Community and Support

The Ruby community is known for its welcoming nature and extensive support systems. This community organizes conferences worldwide, such as RubyConf and RailsConf, where developers gather to share knowledge, discuss advancements, and foster connections within the ecosystem. Online forums, mailing lists, and sites like Stack Overflow and Reddit offer platforms for Rubyists to seek help, collaborate on projects, and contribute to discussions on the language's evolution.

Moreover, the community adheres to a code of conduct known as the Ruby community guidelines, which promotes inclusivity, respect, and collaboration among its members. This atmosphere not only nurtures new developers but also ensures the ongoing health and growth of the Ruby ecosystem.

In summary, the Ruby ecosystem is a comprehensive and dynamic environment that supports the development and execution of Ruby applications. From its powerful interpreter and versatile development tools to its extensive library system, package management, and supportive community, the ecosystem provides everything needed for efficient and enjoyable Ruby programming.

1.3 Ruby Version Management: rbenv and RVM

Managing multiple versions of Ruby on a single system can present significant challenges. Two primary tools have emerged to address these challenges: rbenv and RVM (Ruby Version Manager). These tools enable developers to install, manage, and work with multiple Ruby environments seamlessly. This section will explore the functionalities, installation processes, and basic usage of rbenv and RVM, providing insights into why and when to use each tool.

rbenv

rbenv provides a lightweight and unobtrusive environment for managing Ruby versions. It operates by inserting a directory of shims at the front of the PATH, intercepting Ruby commands and redirecting them to the selected Ruby version.

Installation

Installation of rbenv can be accomplished through several methods, including Homebrew on macOS or git cloning on Linux systems. For example, to install rbenv on macOS:

```
brew install rbenv
```

After installation, initializing rbenv is necessary:

```
rbenv init
```

This command adds the necessary configuration to the shell, enabling rbenv functionality. It is recommended to add this to the shell's startup file.

Usage

To install a new Ruby version using rbenv, use:

```
1   rbenv install 2.7.1
```

Switching the global Ruby version for all shells can be done via:

```
1   rbenv global 2.7.1
```

For project-specific Ruby version management, rbenv facilitates this through a '.ruby-version' file placed in the project's root directory.

RVM

RVM offers a more feature-rich environment compared to rbenv, including gemset management, which allows for separate gem spaces for different projects, reducing the risk of conflict between gem dependencies across projects.

Installation

Installation of RVM is typically performed using the command-line, with the following command for installing the stable release:

```
1   \curl -sSL https://get.rvm.io | bash -s stable
```

Following installation, initializing RVM involves sourcing the RVM script in the shell startup file.

Usage

To install a specific Ruby version using RVM, execute:

```
1   rvm install 2.7.1
```

Setting a default Ruby version is achieved with:

```
1   rvm use 2.7.1 --default
```

RVM's gemset functionality allows for creating isolated environments for gems, preventing conflicts. To create a gemset for a project:

```
1   rvm gemset create projectname
```

Both rbenv and RVM serve vital roles in the Ruby ecosystem for managing multiple Ruby environments. The choice between rbenv and RVM depends on personal or project-specific requirements. rbenv's simplicity and focus on version management make it ideal for those seeking a lightweight solution. In contrast, RVM's comprehensive feature set, including gemset management, offers a more robust tool for handling complex Ruby environments.

1.4   Setting   Up   Your   Development Environment

Setting up a development environment is a critical step in embarking on your Ruby programming journey. A properly configured environment not only facilitates easier development and testing but also ensures that your projects are portable and maintainable. This section will guide you through the essentials for setting up an effective Ruby development environment, including the installation of Ruby, selecting an Integrated Development Environment (IDE) or code editor, and essential tools and plugins that can enhance your development workflow.

Installing Ruby

The first step is to install the Ruby interpreter on your system. There are several ways to install Ruby, including using a version manager, installing from source, or using a package provided by your operating system.

Version Management: rbenv and RVM

For managing different Ruby versions, it is recommended to use a version management tool such as rbenv or RVM. These tools allow you to switch between different Ruby versions easily, which is particularly useful when working on multiple projects that may require different Ruby versions.

To install rbenv, you can use the following commands in your terminal:

```
1  git clone https://github.com/rbenv/rbenv.git ~/.rbenv
2  echo 'export PATH="$HOME/.rbenv/bin:$PATH"' >> ~/.bash_profile
3  ~/.rbenv/bin/rbenv init
```

For installing Ruby using rbenv, you would then proceed with:

```
1  rbenv install 2.7.2
2  rbenv global 2.7.2
```

This will install Ruby version 2.7.2 and set it as the default version globally on your system.

IDEs and Code Editors

Choosing the right IDE or code editor is subjective and depends on personal preferences and the nature of the project. Some popular choices for Ruby development include:

- **Visual Studio Code (VS Code)**: A highly extensible code editor with a vast ecosystem of extensions. For Ruby, the Ruby extension provides enhanced language support including syntax highlighting and debugging capability.

- **RubyMine**: A dedicated Ruby and Rails IDE that offers first-class support for Ruby and Ruby on Rails projects. It includes features such as advanced code analysis, a GUI debugger, and code refactoring support.

- **Sublime Text**: A lightweight and fast code editor with a rich set of plugins available through the Package Control ecosystem. For Ruby, the RubyTest package offers the ability to run Ruby tests directly from within the editor.

Essential Tools and Plugins

To further enhance your Ruby development experience, consider integrating the following tools and plugins into your development environment:

- **RuboCop**: A Ruby static code analyzer, based on the community Ruby style guide. It can enforce many of the guidelines outlined in the style guide and automatically fix many style issues in your code.

- **Pry**: An interactive REPL for Ruby with powerful introspection capabilities, including source code browsing and runtime invocation.

- **Rake**: A make-like build utility for Ruby. It can be used to automate tasks such as building, testing, and deploying applications.

After setting up your Ruby development environment by installing Ruby, choosing an IDE or code editor, and integrating essential tools and plugins, you will be well-equipped to start developing Ruby applications with efficiency and confidence.

1.5 Interactive Ruby with IRB

Interactive Ruby, commonly referred to as IRB, serves as an invaluable tool within the Ruby programming landscape. It is essentially an interactive programming environment that allows for the execution of Ruby commands in real-time, providing instant feedback. This environment is pivotal for experimentation, debugging, and understanding Ruby code.

IRB is included with Ruby's standard distribution, meaning there is no need for additional installation procedures once Ruby is installed on your system. To initiate an IRB session, simply open your command line interface and type `irb`, then press Enter. This action will transition your command line into an interactive Ruby session, indicated by the prompt >>>, which signifies readiness to receive Ruby commands.

An exemplary interaction in IRB may proceed as follows:

```
1   > 2 + 3
```

Upon executing this simple arithmetic operation, the output is immediately presented:

```
=> 5
```

This interaction underscores IRB's utility for quick calculations or script testing without the need to write a complete Ruby script file.

IRB also proves instrumental in exploring Ruby's syntax and experimenting with code snippets. For instance, examining how string concatenation works in Ruby can be done effortlessly within an IRB session:

```
1   > "Hello" + " " + "World!"
```

The concatenated string is returned as:

```
=> "Hello World!"
```

IRB sessions support almost all aspects of Ruby's syntax and capabilities, including variable assignment, method definition, and even the inclusion of modules. For example, defining a simple method to add two numbers can be illustrated as follows:

```
1   > def add(a, b)
2   > return a + b
3   > end
4   > add(5, 3)
```

The method definition is acknowledged, and its invocation yields the expected result:

```
=> 8
```

21

Beyond executing Ruby code, IRB provides additional commands to enhance the interactivity and productivity of your sessions. Some notable commands include:

- `exit` or `quit` - Terminates the IRB session and returns you to the command line.

- `irb_load` - Executes a Ruby script file within the IRB session.

- `irb_save` - Saves the current IRB session's commands to a file.

- `irb_context` - Allows the modification of certain IRB settings such as prompting mode and echo mode.

To further enhance the usability of IRB, several configuration options can be set in the `.irbrc` file, which IRB automatically searches for in your home directory upon startup. This file can contain Ruby code to customize the behavior of your IRB sessions, such as defining default methods or including specific RubyGems.

The utilization of IRB accelerates the learning curve of Ruby programming, offering an immediate and interactive way to experiment with and understand Ruby code. Whether you are a newcomer to Ruby or an experienced developer testing out snippets before integrating them into larger projects, IRB stands as an essential tool in the Ruby ecosystem.

1.6   RubyGems: Discovering   and   Using   Libraries

RubyGems is a package manager for the Ruby programming language that provides a standard format for distributing Ruby programs and libraries. It is an essential tool for any Ruby developer, as it simplifies the process of installing, updating, and managing library dependencies. This system allows developers to share their Ruby libraries (gems) with the wider community, making a vast repository of tools readily available for various applications.

To install a Ruby gem, one uses the `gem` command followed by `install` and the name of the gem. Here's an example that illustrates how to install the Ruby gem named `rails`:

```
1  gem install rails
```

Upon execution, this command contacts the RubyGems website, locates the `rails` gem, and installs it along with its dependencies. The command-line feedback might look something like this:

```
Successfully installed rails-6.0.3.2
Parsing documentation for rails-6.0.3.2
Done installing documentation for rails after 0 seconds
1 gem installed
```

This indicates that the `rails` gem, specifically version 6.0.3.2, was successfully installed, along with the documentation for the gem.

In addition to installing gems, the `gem` command provides functionality for listing installed gems, updating gems, and much more. For example, to list all installed gems, one would use:

```
1  gem list
```

To update a specific gem, simply replace `install` with `update` in the install command. If you want to update all installed gems, you can run:

```
1  gem update
```

Understanding gem dependency is crucial. Some gems rely on other gems to function. When you install a gem, RubyGems will automatically install any necessary dependencies if they are not already installed. This dependency management ensures that all the necessary components are present for a library to function correctly.

RubyGems hosts a vast collection of gems for various purposes—ranging from database drivers, to testing frameworks, to networking libraries, and more. Discovering useful gems for a project can significantly speed up development and extend the functionality of Ruby applications. The RubyGems website (https://rubygems.org) features a search tool that allows developers to search for and explore available gems.

In summary, RubyGems is a powerful and indispensable tool for Ruby developers, facilitating easy management of software libraries and dependencies. It enables the integration of external libraries into projects with minimal effort, promoting code reuse and modularity. With RubyGems, the extensive library of community-contributed gems is just a command away, unlocking nearly limitless potential for Ruby development.

1.7   The Ruby Community: Forums, Conferences, and Projects

The vitality and strength of a programming language are not solely attributed to its syntax or the features it offers but also to the community that surrounds it. Ruby, renowned for its elegance and simplicity, boasts a thriving and welcoming community. This community plays an instrumental role in the development of both novice and seasoned developers through forums, conferences, and collaborative projects.

Forums and Online Discussions

Forums and online discussion platforms serve as the nuclei of the Ruby community, offering spaces for collaboration, learning, and problem-solving. Among the most prominent platforms are:

- Ruby Forum – A dedicated space for discussing all things Ruby. It caters to a range of topics from basic syntax queries to advanced programming concepts.

- Stack Overflow – Although not exclusive to Ruby, Stack Overflow has a vast repository of Ruby-related questions and answers. Its tagging system enables easy navigation and filtering of Ruby-specific inquiries.

- Reddit – The Ruby subreddit (r/ruby) is a vibrant online community for Ruby programmers to share news, tips, and projects.

- GitHub – Beyond hosting code, GitHub facilitates discussion and collaboration on Ruby projects through issues, pull requests, and Gists.

These platforms not only serve as avenues for technical support but also foster a sense of belonging and camaraderie among Ruby developers.

Conferences and Meetups

Ruby conferences and meetups are pivotal in strengthening the community by bringing together developers from various regions and proficiency levels. These events vary from local meetups to international conferences and typically feature talks, workshops, and networking opportunities. Some notable Ruby conferences include:

- RubyConf – An annual, global conference dedicated to Ruby. It encompasses a wide range of topics from the language itself to its applications and the culture surrounding it.

- RailsConf – Focused on Ruby on Rails, this conference addresses the needs and interests of Rails developers with sessions that cover both technical and non-technical subjects.

- RubyKaigi – A conference held in Japan, RubyKaigi presents an opportunity to delve into the Japanese Ruby community, which holds significance due to Ruby's origins.

- Local Meetups – In cities around the world, Ruby users organize regular meetups. These smaller, more informal gatherings allow for deeper discussion and more personalized networking.

Conferences and meetups provide invaluable learning opportunities and foster a sense of solidarity and shared purpose within the Ruby community.

Open Source Projects and Contributions

Ruby's ethos of simplicity and productivity is mirrored in the community's commitment to open source. Numerous Ruby projects are open source, inviting contributions from developers of all skill levels. Contributing to these projects allows developers to:

- Hone their Ruby skills through real-world application.

- Engage with and receive feedback from experienced Rubyists.

- Give back to the community by enhancing and expanding the Ruby ecosystem.

Popular Ruby projects include Rails (a web application framework), Jekyll (a static site generator), and Discourse (a modern forum software). Contribution opportunities range from bug fixes and feature additions to documentation improvements.

The Ruby community, through forums, conferences, and projects, offers an enriching environment for both personal and professional growth. Its inclusive and supportive nature encourages participation and collaboration, making it a cornerstone of the Ruby experience.

1.8 Coding Conventions and Style Guides in Ruby

Coding conventions and style guides play a pivotal role in software development by ensuring code readability, maintainability, and reducing the likelihood of errors. In the Ruby programming community, adherence to commonly accepted conventions and style guides is particularly stressed due to Ruby's philosophy of simplicity and productivity. This section will delineate the key components of Ruby's coding conventions and introduce prominent style guides embraced by Rubyists.

Indentation and Whitespace

Proper indentation and the use of whitespace are fundamental for enhancing the readability of Ruby code. The conventional practice is to use two spaces—no tabs—for indentation. This convention applies to all Ruby code blocks, including methods, class definitions, modules, and conditionals.

```
1  def example_method
2    if condition
3      do_something
4    else
5      do_something_else
6    end
7  end
```

Moreover, it's standard to insert whitespace around operators and after commas to clarify the structure of the code.

```
1  sum = 1 + 2
2  items = [1, 2, 3, 4]
```

Method Names and Variable Naming

Ruby favors the snake_case naming convention for method names and variables. This convention involves writing compound names with lowercase letters, using underscores to separate words.

```
1  employee_name = "John Doe"
2  def calculate_salary
3    # Method body
4  end
```

Comments and Documentation

Ruby programmers are encouraged to comment their code adequately. Comments should clarify "why" something is done rather than "what" is being done, as the code itself should be self-explanatory for the latter. The use of YARD (Yay! A Ruby Documentation Tool) annotations for documentation is also encouraged for providing a structured and comprehensive documentation that can be easily converted to HTML.

```ruby
1  # Calculates and returns the sum of two numbers
2  # @param [Integer] num1 The first number
3  # @param [Integer] num2 The second number
4  # @return [Integer] The sum of num1 and num2
5  def sum(num1, num2)
6    num1 + num2
7  end
```

Control Structures

Ruby allows for various control structures, but the use of modifier forms is recommended for single-line bodies to make the code succinct and more readable.

```ruby
1  do_something if condition
2
3  items.each { |item| puts item } if items.any?
```

Ruby Style Guides

Several Ruby style guides provide comprehensive descriptions of best practices. The most renowned among these is the Ruby Style Guide by Bozhidar Batsov, which is widely consulted by Ruby programmers. It includes guidelines covering syntax, naming, commenting, and much more. This style guide, alongside others like Airbnb's Ruby Style Guide, helps programmers write Ruby code that is not only functional but also clean and consistent with Ruby's philosophy.

Adhering to coding conventions and style guides in Ruby is essential for writing elegant, readable, and maintainable code. By following the practices outlined above and consulting established style guides, Ruby programmers can ensure that their code aligns with the community's standards and values.

Chapter 2

Ruby Basics: Syntax, Data Types, and Variables

This chapter delves into the foundational elements that constitute the Ruby programming language, starting with its syntax which is designed for clarity and minimalism. It examines Ruby's primary data types, including numbers, strings, and booleans, and explores how variables are used to store information. The discussion extends to mutable and immutable objects, operators, and expressions, providing a comprehensive understanding of how Ruby handles basic programming constructs and paving the way for more complex topics.

2.1 The Basic Structure of a Ruby Program

Understanding the fundamental structure of a Ruby program is essential for grasping the language's simplicity and elegance. A Ruby program consists of a sequence of declarations and instructions that the Ruby interpreter processes. These elements can include variable assignments, method definitions, control structures, and more, all following a syntax that emphasizes human

31

readability.

At its core, a Ruby script is a text file with the '.rb' extension, containing executable code. Ruby executes this code sequentially, line by line, from the top of the file to the bottom, unless the flow is explicitly altered through control structures or method calls.

Let's begin with a simple example that prints "Hello, world!" to the console:

```
1  puts "Hello, world!"
```

This one-liner encapsulates the beauty of Ruby's syntax — straightforward and concise. The 'puts' method prints its argument, followed by a newline, to the console.

Expanding on this foundation, let's examine a typical structure of a more complex Ruby program. A well-organized Ruby program often starts with a shebang line, followed by file-level documentation, required libraries/modules (using 'require' or 'require_relative'), class and module definitions, and finally, executable code.

Here is a basic template:

```
1   #!/usr/bin/env ruby
2
3   # This is a simple Ruby program
4
5   require 'json'
6
7   class Greeter
8     def initialize(name)
9       @name = name
10    end
11
12    def greet
13      puts "Hello, #{@name}!"
14    end
15  end
16
17  greeter = Greeter.new("Alice")
18  greeter.greet
```

Breaking down this template, we note the following:

- The first line, often referred to as the shebang, tells the system that this script should be executed using the Ruby interpreter.

This line is crucial for scripts intended to be run directly from a Unix-like command line.

- Following the shebang, comments can be used to provide file-level documentation. Comments in Ruby begin with the '#' character and extend to the end of the line.

- The 'require' statement is used to include external modules and libraries. This enhances the functionality of the program by allowing it to leverage a wide array of existing Ruby gems and libraries.

- Class definitions start with the keyword 'class', followed by the class name. In Ruby, class names must begin with a capital letter. Methods are defined within classes using the 'def' keyword, and instance variables, which store object state, are prefixed with '@'.

- The executable portion of the script typically follows the class and module definitions. In this example, an instance of the 'Greeter' class is created, and its 'greet' method is called.

Understanding these components of a Ruby program's structure provides a solid foundation for constructing well-organized, readable, and maintainable Ruby applications. As with any programming language, mastering the basics of program structure is crucial for effective coding and debugging.

2.2 Variables and Assignment

In this section, we will discuss the core concepts of variables and how assignment works in Ruby. Variables can be thought of as named containers that store information or data which can later be retrieved, manipulated, or modified. Ruby, being a dynamic and strongly typed language, does not require explicit declaration of variable data types. The type is inferred at runtime based on the value assigned to the variable.

Declaration and Assignment

In Ruby, variables are declared the moment you assign a value to them using the equals sign =. This is known as the assignment operator.

```
1  my_number = 10
2  greeting = "Hello, Ruby!"
3  is_valid = true
```

In the examples above, my_number is assigned an integer value of 10, greeting is assigned a string value of "Hello, Ruby!", and is_valid is assigned a boolean value of true. The process of assignment associates a name (for instance, my_number) with a memory location that holds the value (10 in this case). Whenever my_number is used, Ruby will refer to the memory location and work with the value stored there.

Variable Naming Conventions

Ruby has a simple yet strict set of rules for naming variables:

- Variable names must begin with a lowercase letter or an underscore.

- After the first character, variable names can include letters, digits, or underscores.

- Variable names are case-sensitive. For example, myVar and myvar would be considered two distinct variables.

Following these conventions is crucial for clear and maintainable code. Additionally, it is a common practice to use snake_case for variable names; for instance, customer_name or total_amount.

Dynamic Typing and Mutable Objects

Ruby's dynamic typing means that a variable can be reassigned to hold data of a different type without any issues.

```
1  x = 100 # Initially, x is an Integer
2  x = "Ruby" # Now, x is a String
```

The concept of mutable objects in Ruby allows for the modification of an object without changing the memory address to which the variable points. For instance, when manipulating strings or arrays, the changes happen in place.

```
1  names = ["Alice", "Bob"]
2  names << "Charlie" # names now includes "Charlie"
```

However, it's important to understand that when you reassign a variable, you are not mutating the object it points to but instead pointing the variable to a new object (or place in memory).

Parallel Assignment

Ruby provides a convenient way to assign values to multiple variables in a single statement, known as parallel assignment.

```
1  a, b, c = 10, 20, 30
```

This feature can be particularly useful for swapping the values of two variables without requiring a temporary third variable.

```
1  a, b = b, a
```

In the example above, the values of a and b are swapped in a concise and readable manner.

Understanding variables and assignment is foundational to mastering Ruby, as they are used in every aspect of Ruby programming. With this knowledge, we can move on to explore Ruby's data types and how they interact with variables and assignment.

2.3 Data Types: Numbers, Strings, and Booleans

In this section, we will discuss the fundamental data types in Ruby: numbers, strings, and booleans. These data types are the building blocks for constructing more complex data structures and are essential for performing most programming tasks in Ruby.

Numbers

Ruby supports a wide range of numbers, including integers and floating-point numbers. Integer data types represent whole numbers, either positive or negative. Floating-point numbers, on the other hand, are used to represent decimal numbers or numbers that require a higher degree of precision.

An example of an integer assignment in Ruby is as follows:

```
1  age = 30
```

For floating-point numbers, an example would be:

```
1  temperature = 98.6
```

Ruby automatically determines the type of the number based on its value. If a number includes a decimal point, Ruby treats it as a floating-point number.

Strings

Strings in Ruby are sequences of characters enclosed in quotes. Ruby supports both single (') and double (") quotes for defining strings. The main difference between them is that double quotes allow for string interpolation and the inclusion of escape sequences.

An example of a simple string is:

```
1  greeting = "Hello, World!"
```

String interpolation allows for the insertion of Ruby code within a string. The code is executed, and its result is included in the string. An example is:

```
1  name = "Alice"
2  greeting = "Hello, #{name}!"
```

The output of the greeting variable would now be "Hello, Alice!".

Booleans

Booleans in Ruby are represented by just two values: true and false. Unlike some other programming languages, Ruby does not treat numbers, strings, or 'nil' as boolean values. The only instances that evaluate to false are the boolean false itself and 'nil'.

A boolean assignment can look like this:

```
1  is_raining = true
```

Ruby's booleans are pivotal in control flow and logical operations, which are discussed in later sections.

Converting Between Number Types

Occasionally, it may be necessary to convert between integer and floating-point numbers. Ruby provides methods for these conversions: to_i for converting to an integer and to_f for converting to a floating-point number.

Here is an example of converting a string representing a number to an integer and a floating-point number:

```
1  number_str = "10"
2  number_int = number_str.to_i
3  number_float = number_str.to_f
```

The variable number_int would now hold the integer 10, while number_float would hold the floating-point number 10.0.

This section has covered the basics of numbers, strings, and booleans in Ruby. Understanding these data types and how to manipulate them is fundamental to becoming proficient in Ruby programming.

2.4   Mutable vs Immutable Objects

Understanding the distinction between mutable and immutable objects is central to grasping the core mechanics of Ruby, as well as many other programming languages. This concept is pivotal because it affects how data stored in memory can be manipulated and managed throughout the execution of a program.

In Ruby, an object's mutability is determined by its ability to change after it has been instantiated. Mutable objects can have their state or content modified post-creation, while immutable objects cannot. This characteristic has profound implications for how variables and objects interact, particularly when considering Ruby's approach to variable assignment and object manipulation.

Characteristics of Mutable Objects

Mutable objects in Ruby encompass arrays, hashes, and instances of custom classes, amongst others. These objects can be altered after their creation through methods that modify their content or state. For instance:

```
1  names = ['Alice', 'Bob']
2  names.push('Charlie') # Adds 'Charlie' to the array
```

In the above example, the array names is mutated by adding another element ('Charlie') using the push method. This mutability feature allows for flexible manipulation of the object's content without needing to create a new object.

Characteristics of Immutable Objects

On the other hand, immutable objects in Ruby include integers, floats, symbols, and, notably, strings (inversions prior to Ruby 2.4). Once an immutable object is created, its value or state cannot be altered. Instead, any action that appears to modify an immutable object results in the creation of a new object. Consider the following example:

```
1  name = "Alice"
2  another_name = name.upcase # Creates a new string "ALICE"
```

The upcase method does not mutate the original string; rather, it returns a new string with all uppercase letters. The original string, referenced by name, remains unchanged. This demonstrates the immutable nature of strings (in Ruby versions prior to 2.4).

Mutability and Variable Assignment

Variable assignment in Ruby further elucidates the distinction between mutable and immutable objects. When a variable is assigned the value of another variable, both variables point to the same object in memory if that object is immutable. However, if the object is mutable, operations that modify the object through one of the variables will reflect when accessed via the other variable. Consider:

```
1  original = ['apple', 'banana']
2  copy = original
3  copy.push('carrot') # Mutates the object
4  puts original.inspect # Output: ["apple", "banana", "carrot"]
```

The push operation on copy also affects original because both variables reference the same mutable object (the array). This behavior underscores the importance of understanding object mutability in Ruby, as it influences how data is manipulated and managed across a program.

Distinguishing between mutable and immutable objects in Ruby is crucial for effective programming. This knowledge informs the management of variable assignments, the manipulation of objects, and the overall structure of Ruby programs. It allows developers to make informed decisions about data handling, ensuring code efficiency, and integrity.

2.5   Symbols: What They Are and How to Use Them

Symbols in Ruby hold a unique position, different from other data types such as numbers, strings, or booleans. They are lightweight, immutable identifiers used for conveying meaning in a more efficient manner than strings. Understanding symbols is crucial for efficient Ruby programming, especially when dealing with hash keys or method names.

A symbol in Ruby is created by prefixing a word with a colon (:). For example, :username and :password are symbols.

```
:my_symbol
:user_id
:data
```

Unlike strings, symbols of the same name are initialized and exist in memory only once. This characteristic makes symbols highly memory-efficient and faster to compare than strings, which makes them an ideal choice for identifiers, keys in hashes, or any place where distinctive names are required but string functionality is not.

To illustrate the difference in object allocation between strings and symbols, consider the following Ruby code:

```
puts "string".object_id
puts "string".object_id
puts :symbol.object_id
puts :symbol.object_id
```

The output of the above code will show different object IDs for the strings but the same object ID for the symbol:

70157165670380

This example clearly demonstrates how multiple instances of a string result in different objects, whereas a symbol remains a single object across its usage, thereby conserving memory.

Using Symbols

Symbols are most commonly used as keys in hashes due to their efficiency. With symbols, Ruby does not need to re-evaluate the hash key string each time it is accessed; instead, it can directly reference the immutable symbol, leading to faster key lookup times.

```
1  user_data = { :name => "John Doe", :age => 30 }
2  puts user_data[:name]
```

Here, :name and :age are symbols used as keys in the user_data hash. The use of symbols as keys is a common practice in Ruby, making code more performance-oriented and memory-efficient.

Moreover, symbols can be used in method names and object attributes. This makes code not only cleaner but also slightly faster in execution when compared to strings.

In summary, symbols serve as a powerful construct in Ruby for representing names and some strings inside a program. They are immutable, thereby guaranteeing that their state cannot be altered once created. This immutability, coupled with their single instance in memory, renders symbols a preferred choice for hash keys, method names, and more. The memory efficiency and speed advantage of symbols are particularly noticeable in large-scale Ruby applications, where performance optimization is crucial.

2.6   Operators and Expressions

Operators are fundamental tools in Ruby that allow you to perform various operations on one or more objects. An expression, on the

41

other hand, is a combination of one or more operators and operands (variables, literals, method calls) that Ruby evaluates to produce another value. This section covers the types of operators Ruby supports and illustrates how expressions are formed and evaluated.

Types of Operators

Ruby supports a variety of operators, classified into the following categories:

- Arithmetic Operators
- Comparison Operators
- Assignment Operators
- Logical Operators
- Bitwise Operators
- Range Operators

Each category plays a distinct role in Ruby expressions, influencing how values are manipulated, compared, assigned, and logical decisions are made.

Arithmetic Operators

Arithmetic operators include + (addition), - (subtraction), * (multiplication), / (division), and % (modulo). Ruby also provides the ** operator for exponentiation.

For instance, adding two numbers in Ruby can be accomplished with the following code:

```
1   sum = 5 + 3
```

Which would result in:

8

Comparison Operators

Comparison operators compare two values and return a boolean value, either true or false. These include == (equal), != (not equal), > (greater than), < (less than), >= (greater than or equal to), and <= (less than or equal to).

A simple comparison might look like this:

```
1  is_greater = 10 > 5
```

Yielding a boolean value:

```
true
```

Assignment Operators

Assignment operators are used to assign values to variables. The most basic assignment operator is =. Ruby also provides compound assignment operators that combine arithmetic or bitwise operations with assignment, such as +=, -=, *=, and /=.

```
1  x = 10
2  x += 2
```

After execution, x would have the value:

```
12
```

Logical Operators

Logical operators include and (also represented as &&), or (also represented as ||), and not (also represented as !). These operators are used to combine multiple conditions in control structures.

```
1  is_adult = true
2  has_permission = false
3  can_enter = is_adult && has_permission
```

The can_enter variable evaluates to:

```
false
```

Bitwise Operators

Bitwise operators act on the binary representations of integers, performing operations bit by bit. These include & (AND), | (OR), ̂ (XOR), and ̃ (NOT).

```
1    result = 12 & 5
```

Which evaluates to:

```
4
```

Range Operators

Ruby provides two range operators: .. (inclusive) and ... (exclusive), which are used to create ranges of values. These ranges can be iterated over or used to create subsets of arrays and other enumerable types.

```
1    inclusive_range = (1..5).to_a
2    exclusive_range = (1...5).to_a
```

The ranges convert to arrays as follows:

```
[1, 2, 3, 4, 5]
[1, 2, 3, 4]
```

Evaluating Expressions

An expression in Ruby is evaluated based on the precedence of its operators. Operators with higher precedence are evaluated before those with lower precedence. Parentheses can be used to alter the default precedence and group parts of an expression explicitly.

For complex expressions involving multiple types of operators, Ruby follows a specific order of operations, akin to the BODMAS rule in mathematics. It is crucial to understand this order to predict the outcome of expressions accurately.

Consider the following expression:

```
1   result = 1 + 2 * 3 / 4.0
```

The multiplication and division have higher precedence than addition, so Ruby evaluates the expression in the order:

```
1   result = 1 + (2 * 3) / 4.0
```

Resulting in:

2.5

Operators and expressions are the building blocks of Ruby programs, allowing for the manipulation and comparison of data, the assignment of values, the execution of logical operations, and the creation of ranges. Understanding these concepts is essential for developing efficient and effective Ruby code.

2.7   Comments and Documentation

Comments in Ruby, as in many programming languages, serve the critical function of providing explanations or annotations within the code.   They are indispensable for maintaining clear and understandable codebases, especially in collaborative environments or for future reference.

In Ruby, comments begin with the # symbol and extend to the end of the line. Anything following the # symbol on the same line is ignored by the Ruby interpreter. This property is utilized to add notes or disable code temporarily without deleting it. Consider the following example:

```
1   # This is a single-line comment in Ruby
2   puts "Hello, world!" # This comment is inline with code
```

For more extensive documentation or explanations, Ruby conveniently allows the creation of block comments, which can span multiple lines without the need to prefix each line with the # symbol.   This is achieved using the =begin and =end syntax. Everything between these two keywords is considered a comment:

45

```
1   =begin
2   This is a block comment in Ruby
3   which spans multiple lines.
4   These kinds of comments are ideal for
5   providing detailed documentation at the beginning of files
6   or explaining complex algorithms.
7   =end
8   puts "Block comments are above this line."
```

It is worth noting that block comments should be used sparingly, as they can sometimes obfuscate the structure of the code if overused. Inline and single-line comments are generally preferred for their brevity and direct association with specific lines of code.

Documentation in Ruby can also be generated automatically using tools such as RDoc. RDoc processes Ruby source files to extract documentation from comments and generate HTML (or other formats) documentation. To effectively utilize RDoc, comments should be written above method definitions or class declarations, following specific conventions, such as starting a comment with the method name, followed by a description, parameters, and return values:

```
1    # Calculates the sum of two numbers
2    #
3    # Parameters:
4    # a:: Number to be added to b
5    # b:: Number to be added to a
6    #
7    # Returns:
8    # Sum of a and b
9    def sum(a, b)
10     a + b
11   end
```

This method documentation is straightforward, providing clear information about the purpose of the method, its parameters, and what it returns.

In summary, properly commenting code and following documentation guidelines are fundamental practices in Ruby programming. They aid in maintaining readable, understandable, and maintainable code, which is crucial for both individual projects and collaborative efforts. Leveraging comments judiciously and adopting tools like RDoc for creating documentation can significantly enhance the development process and the quality of the codebase.

2.8   Conditional Expressions: if, unless, case

Conditional expressions are fundamental in Ruby, allowing for decision-making in the code. Ruby provides several conditional structures, namely if, unless, and case, each serving unique purposes and scenarios.

The if Statement

The if statement evaluates a condition, executing a block of code only if the condition is true. The basic syntax is as follows:

```
1  if condition
2    # block of code to execute if the condition is true
3  end
```

For instance, checking if a number is positive can be implemented like this:

```
1  if number > 0
2    puts "The number is positive."
3  end
```

Ruby also supports else and elsif constructs for multiple conditions:

```
1  if number > 0
2    puts "The number is positive."
3  elsif number < 0
4    puts "The number is negative."
5  else
6    puts "The number is zero."
7  end
```

The `unless` Statement

An often clearer alternative to `if !condition` is `unless`, which executes code only if the condition is false. Its basic structure is:

```
unless condition
  # block of code to execute if the condition is false
end
```

For instance, to check if a list is not empty before performing an operation:

```
unless list.empty?
  list.each do |item|
    puts item
  end
end
```

Similar to `if`, `unless` also supports `else`:

```
unless number >= 0
  puts "The number is negative."
else
  puts "The number is positive or zero."
end
```

The `case` Statement

When dealing with multiple conditions leading to different outcomes, a case statement is more efficient and readable than multiple `if elsif` conditions. The syntax is:

```
case variable
when condition1
  # block of code for condition1
when condition2
  # block of code for condition2
else
  # block of code if none of the conditions match
end
```

For example, categorizing a test score can be neatly done with:

```
case score
when 90..100
  grade = "A"
```

```
 4   when 80...90
 5     grade = "B"
 6   when 70...80
 7     grade = "C"
 8   else
 9     grade = "F"
10   end
11
12   puts "Your grade is #{grade}."
```

case statements are particularly powerful when combined with Ruby's range objects (. . and . . .) for defining conditions.

Comparing Equality and Comparing Identity in case Expressions

An essential distinction in case statements is between comparing equality (==) and comparing object identity (equal?). The case statement uses == by default for comparison, not equal?, meaning it checks if the values are the same, not if they are the same object in memory.

However, one can explicitly use equal? in when conditions when necessary:

```
1   object = some_object # an arbitrary object
2   case object
3   when ->(x) { x.equal?(expected_object) }
4     puts "Object identity matches."
5   else
6     puts "Different objects."
7   end
```

This uses a lambda to compare the object identity within a when condition, showcasing the flexibility of Ruby's case expressions.

In addition to these fundamental conditional structures, Ruby offers syntactic sugar such as statement modifiers (if and unless at the end of a statement) and ternary operators for inline conditions. These features enhance Ruby's expressiveness and readability, making it a powerful language for both beginners and experienced programmers.

2.9   Methods: Defining and Invoking

Methods in Ruby are a fundamental construct that enable code reusability and organization. By definition, a method is a block of code designed to perform a specific task. This section will elucidate the process of defining and invoking methods in Ruby, detailing the syntax, parameters, return values, and common practices associated with methods.

Defining Methods

To define a method in Ruby, the keyword def is utilized, followed by the method name and an optional list of parameters. The block of code to be executed is enclosed within this structure and ends with the keyword end. The general syntax is as follows:

```
1  def method_name(parameter1, parameter2)
2    # Code block to be executed
3  end
```

It is imperative to adhere to naming conventions for methods, which typically involve using snake_case for the method name.

A method can return a value explicitly using the return keyword or implicitly, where the last evaluated expression's result is returned. For instance:

```
1  def sum(a, b)
2    return a + b
3  end
4
5  def greeting(name)
6    "Hello, #{name}"
7  end
```

In the sum method, the return keyword explicitly returns the sum of a and b. Conversely, the greeting method returns the string "Hello, #name" implicitly, without explicitly using the return keyword.

Invoking Methods

Once defined, methods can be invoked or called using their name followed by parentheses containing any arguments to be passed. If a method does not require any parameters, the parentheses can be omitted. However, including them is a common practice for clarity.

```
1  puts sum(2, 3) # Outputs: 5
2
3  puts greeting("Alice") # Outputs: Hello, Alice
```

Method Parameters

Ruby methods can accept a range of parameters, including mandatory parameters, optional parameters with default values, and variable-length arguments, among others.   Here is how different types of parameters can be deployed:

- **Mandatory Parameters:** These parameters must be provided when the method is called. The absence of these arguments will result in an error.

- **Optional Parameters:** Defined by assigning a default value in the method definition, these parameters are not mandatory. If not provided, the default value is used.

- **Variable-Length Arguments:** Also known as splat parameters, denoted by an asterisk (*) before the parameter name, allow passing an arbitrary number of arguments as an array.

```
1  def info(name, age = 30, *hobbies)
2    "Name: #{name}, Age: #{age}, Hobbies: #{hobbies.join(', ')}"
3  end
4
5  puts info("John", 25, "Swimming", "Reading")
6  # Outputs: Name: John, Age: 25, Hobbies: Swimming, Reading
7
8  puts info("Jane")
9  # Outputs: Name: Jane, Age: 30, Hobbies:
```

Method Invocations as Arguments

Methods in Ruby can be invoked with other method calls as arguments. This allows for compact and expressive code constructs. For example:

```
def square(x)
  x * x
end

def add(a, b)
  a + b
end

puts add(square(2), square(3)) # Outputs: 13
```

In this instance, the add method is invoked with the results of the square method calls as its arguments.

Ruby methods are versatile constructs that organize code into reusable blocks for specific tasks. Understanding the syntax and best practices surrounding method definition and invocation is crucial for writing clean and efficient Ruby code. This section has explored the essentials of methods, including definition, parameter handling, and invocation techniques, providing a solid foundation for further exploration of Ruby's capabilities.

2.10 Converting Between Different Data Types

Converting between different data types is an essential operation in Ruby, as it allows for flexible manipulation and handling of data. Ruby provides straightforward methods for these conversions, which can be invaluable in situations where operations require data of a specific type.

Converting to Strings

To convert any object to a string, Ruby uses the .to_s method. This method is called on the variable that needs conversion. For instance, converting a number to a string is as follows:

```
1  age = 30
2  age_string = age.to_s
```

The variable age_string will now contain the value "30", which is a string representation of the integer 30.

Converting to Integers

Similarly, Ruby facilitates converting other data types into integers using the .to_i method. This conversion is particularly useful when dealing with strings that represent numerical values:

```
1  number_string = "42"
2  number = number_string.to_i
```

After execution, the variable number will hold the integer value 42.

Converting to Floats

For conversions to floating-point numbers, Ruby provides the .to_f method. This is useful when precision is necessary for operations like division:

```
1  string = "3.14"
2  pi = string.to_f
```

The pi variable would now contain the float value 3.14.

Boolean Conversions

Ruby does not provide direct methods like .to_b for converting data types to booleans. Instead, it follows a simple rule: all values are inherently true, except for `nil` and `false`. Therefore, any conversion to a boolean is based on this principle rather than a method call.

Complex Conversions

In some cases, conversions might not be straightforward, especially when dealing with custom objects or unusual data structures. For these scenarios, Ruby allows the definition of custom to_ methods within the class to handle specific conversion logic.

```
1   class Person
2     attr_accessor :name
3
4     def initialize(name)
5       @name = name
6     end
7
8     def to_s
9       @name
10     end
11   end
12
13   person = Person.new("Alice")
14   puts person.to_s
```

In the example above, a `Person` object is converted to a string using a custom `to_s` method, which returns the person's name.

Practical Considerations

When converting between data types, it is crucial to consider the context and ensure the conversion logic aligns with the expectations of the program's logic. Loss of information can occur, especially when converting from a type with a larger range (e.g., float) to a type with a smaller range (e.g., integer), potentially leading to subtle bugs. Therefore, carefully designing conversion strategies is essential for robust and error-free code.

Ruby's data type conversion methods (`.to_s`, `.to_i`, and `.to_f`) are straightforward and provide a solid foundation for handling type conversions. However, understanding the implications of these conversions and implementing custom conversion methods when necessary can significantly enhance the flexibility and reliability of Ruby applications.

This detailed explanation covers the key aspects of converting between different data types in Ruby, focusing on built-in methods and the considerations necessary for custom conversions.

2.11 Understanding Scope and Visibility

In Ruby, scope determines the accessibility of variables, and visibility dictates how and where we can access those variables within our code. Understanding these concepts is crucial because they directly influence the behavior of our program and help maintain its structure and security.

Scope in Ruby

Scope in Ruby is divided into four main types: local, global, instance, and class. Each type has its set of rules regarding where the variables can be accessed.

- Local Variables: Defined by a name starting with a lowercase letter or an underscore. Their scope is limited to the block, method, class, or module in which they are defined. They are not accessible outside their defining context.

- Global Variables: Prefixed with a $ symbol. These variables are accessible from anywhere within the Ruby program, making them highly flexible but also potentially risky to use due to their unrestricted scope.

- Instance Variables: Begin with an @ symbol. These are available across different methods within the same instance of a class, making them essential for instance-specific behavior and states.

- Class Variables: Start with a double at symbol @@. They are shared across all instances of a class and even subclasses, which means they can be accessed within class methods and instance methods alike.

Visibility in Ruby

Ruby's methods visibility is categorized into three groups: public, protected, and private.

- Public Methods: Can be called by any other object. By default, instance methods are public except for 'initialize', which is always private.

- Protected Methods: Can only be called by objects of the same class or subclasses. Use of protected methods is restricted to within the class definition and comparing objects of the same class.

- Private Methods: Cannot be called with an explicit receiver. This means you cannot specify the object to which the method should send the message, making these methods strictly available to the object itself.

To change a method's visibility, Ruby provides three key method calls: `public`, `protected`, and `private`. These can be used to alter the default visibility. An example to illustrate changing method visibility is shown below:

```
1   class Example
2
3     # Initially, this method is public
4     def public_method
5       puts "I'm a public method!"
6     end
7
8     private
9
10    def private_method
11      puts "I'm a private method!"
12    end
13
14  end
15
16  # Attempting to call the private method will result in an error
```

```
17  example = Example.new
18  example.public_method # This works fine
19  example.private_method # This raises an error
```

Note: Attempting to access a private method from outside the instance will raise a NoMethodError.

Scope Resolution with Constants

Constants in Ruby, which are supposed to hold values that never change, have their own scope rules. Defined with a name starting with an uppercase letter, constants are accessible within the class or module in which they are defined, and their visibility can be controlled using the private_constant and public_constant methods.

```
1  class MyClass
2    MY_CONSTANT = 'I am accessible everywhere within MyClass'
3
4    private_constant :MY_CONSTANT
5  end
6
7  puts MyClass::MY_CONSTANT
8  # This will raise a NameError: private constant MyClass::MY_CONSTANT accessed
```

The scope and visibility mechanisms in Ruby are foundational to structuring a program that not only functions correctly but also adheres to good practices of encapsulation and data protection. By carefully selecting the scope and visibility for variables and methods, developers can create robust, secure, and maintainable programs.

Chapter 3

Control Structures: Conditionals, Loops, and Iterators

In this chapter, we focus on Ruby's control structures, which are vital for creating logical flow and repetition within programs. It covers conditional statements like if, unless, and case expressions, and introduces looping constructs including while, until, and for loops, as well as iterator methods such as each and times. Through these mechanisms, Ruby offers flexible ways to control program execution, allowing developers to write concise, readable code that efficiently handles repetitive tasks and decision-making processes.

3.1 Understanding Boolean Expressions

In this section, we will examine the fundamental concept underlying most control structures in Ruby: Boolean expressions. Boolean expressions evaluate to either true or false, which are the only two values possible in Boolean logic. These expressions are the cornerstone of decision-making in programming, enabling the execution of code blocks based on certain conditions.

The simplest form of a Boolean expression is a comparison between two values. Ruby provides a variety of comparison operators to facilitate this:

- == (equals)

- != (not equals)

- > (greater than)

- < (less than)

- >= (greater than or equal to)

- <= (less than or equal to)

For example, evaluating the expression 5 > 3 would yield true, as 5 is indeed greater than 3.

Boolean expressions can also involve logical operators that combine or negate the results of other Boolean expressions. The primary logical operators in Ruby are:

- ! (logical NOT): Inverts the truth value of its operand.

- && (logical AND): Evaluates to true if both operands are true.

- || (logical OR): Evaluates to true if at least one of the operands is true.

For instance, the expression (5 > 3) && (2 == 2) combines two simple expressions using the && operator and evaluates to true because both individual conditions are true.

Moreover, Ruby expressions that are not explicitly Boolean can still be used in a Boolean context, following the principle of truthiness. In Ruby, every value except false and nil is considered true when evaluated in a Boolean context. This characteristic allows for more flexibility in writing conditions. Consider the following if statement:

```
1  if x
2    puts "x is considered true!"
3  end
```

In this code snippet, if x holds any value other than `false` or `nil`, the message will be printed. This demonstrates how Ruby's conditional expressions leverage the concept of truthiness, simplifying certain types of logic.

Understanding Boolean expressions is critical not only for making decisions within your program but also for controlling the flow of execution in loops and iterators, topics which will be explored further in subsequent sections. By mastering these expressions, developers can write more concise, logical, and readable Ruby code.

3.2   The If, Else, and Elsif Statements

Ruby's control structures are essential for imparting a logical flow to your program, with conditional statements playing a central role in decision-making processes.   Conditional statements evaluate whether a given condition is true or false, and then execute a corresponding block of code based on the evaluation's outcome. The `if`, `else`, and `elsif` statements in Ruby offer a straightforward yet powerful way to control the flow of a program.

The `if` Statement

The `if` statement evaluates a condition and executes a block of code if the condition is true. The basic syntax of an `if` statement is as follows:

```
1  if condition
2    # code to be executed if condition is true
3  end
```

For example, to print "Hello, world!" if a variable x is greater than 10, you would write:

```
1  x = 11
```

```
2  if x > 10
3    puts "Hello, world!"
4  end
```

The else Statement

The else statement provides a block of code that will be executed if the condition in the if statement is evaluated to false. The else statement helps in defining an alternative path of execution. The syntax is as follows:

```
1  if condition
2    # code to be executed if condition is true
3  else
4    # code to be executed if condition is false
5  end
```

For instance, to print "x is greater than 10" if x is greater than 10, and "x is 10 or less" otherwise, the code would look as follows:

```
1  x = 9
2  if x > 10
3    puts "x is greater than 10"
4  else
5    puts "x is 10 or less"
6  end
```

The elsif Statement

When there are multiple conditions to evaluate, the elsif statement can be used to add additional conditions to the if statement. The elsif (short for "else if") allows for specifying several alternative conditions, each with its corresponding block of code to be executed if that condition is true. The syntax incorporates multiple elsif statements as follows:

```
1  if condition1
2    # code to be executed if condition1 is true
3  elsif condition2
4    # code to be executed if condition2 is true
5  else
6    # code to be executed if none of the above conditions are true
7  end
```

An example usage of `elsif` to check the size category of a number could be:

```
1   number = 15
2   if number < 10
3     puts "The number is small"
4   elsif number >= 10 && number <= 20
5     puts "The number is medium"
6   else
7     puts "The number is large"
8   end
```

The `if`, `else`, and `elsif` statements serve as the foundation for implementing decision-making logic in a Ruby program. Through these constructs, developers can direct the flow of execution based on various conditions, making the code both flexible and powerful.

3.3   Loops in Ruby: while and until

Loops are indispensable in any programming language, offering a way to repeatedly execute a block of code as long as a certain condition is true. Ruby, with its elegant syntax, provides several looping constructs, among which the `while` and `until` loops are the most frequently used for conditional looping. These loops enable developers to execute code blocks multiple times based on dynamic conditions, enhancing the flexibility and power of Ruby scripts.

The while Loop

The `while` loop in Ruby iterates through a block of code as long as the specified condition evaluates to true. The basic syntax of a `while` loop is as follows:

```
1   while condition
2     # code to be executed
3   end
```

The condition is evaluated before each iteration, and if it's true, the code within the loop is executed. This process repeats until the condition becomes false.

Here is a practical example demonstrating the use of a `while` loop to print numbers from 1 to 5:

```
1  x = 1
2  while x <= 5
3    puts x
4    x += 1
5  end
```

The output for this code will be:

```
1
2
3
4
5
```

This example initializes a variable x with the value 1 and increments it by 1 in each iteration of the loop. The loop continues as long as x is less than or equal to 5.

The until Loop

Conversely, the `until` loop in Ruby functions as a complement to the `while` loop. It performs the iteration of a block of code until a specified condition evaluates to true. Essentially, the `until` loop continues to run as long as the condition is false. The syntax for an `until` loop is similar to that of a `while` loop but uses the keyword `until`:

```
1  until condition
2    # code to be executed
3  end
```

Here's how to use an `until` loop to achieve the same result as the previous example:

```
1  x = 1
2  until x > 5
3    puts x
4    x += 1
5  end
```

This code snippet will produce exactly the same output as the `while` loop example.

Both the `while` and `until` loops offer Ruby developers a straightforward method to execute repetitive tasks with minimal code. However, it's crucial to ensure that the condition eventually becomes false to avoid infinite loops, which can cause a program to hang or crash.

To further control the execution within these loops, Ruby offers the `break`, `next`, and `redo` keywords, which can be used to exit the loop, skip to the next iteration, or redo the current iteration, respectively. These control flow mechanisms add another layer of flexibility to Ruby's looping constructs.

3.4 Controlling Loops with break, next, and redo

In this section, we will discuss the mechanisms provided by Ruby to control the flow of loops beyond their basic iteration patterns. Specifically, we will examine the use of `break`, `next`, and `redo` keywords within looping constructs, which allow for more dynamic loop management. Understanding these controls is crucial for writing efficient and flexible loop structures that can adapt to a variety of runtime conditions.

break: The `break` keyword is used to exit a loop immediately, disregarding the loop's normal termination condition. It is particularly useful when some external condition is met, rendering further iterations unnecessary or undesirable. Upon encountering a `break`, Ruby terminates the nearest enclosing loop and proceeds with the execution of the code that follows the loop.

Consider the following example where `break` is used to exit a loop when a certain condition is met:

```
1  numbers = [1, 2, 3, 4, 5, 6]
2  numbers.each do |number|
3    break if number > 4
4    puts number
5  end
```

1

```
2
3
4
```

In the example above, the loop iterates over the elements of the array until it encounters a number greater than 4, at which point it executes the break command and exits the loop immediately.

next: The next keyword allows the loop to skip the remainder of the code block for the current iteration and proceed directly to the next iteration. This is useful for filtering out certain conditions within a loop without terminating the loop entirely.

Here is an example of how next can be used within a loop:

```
1  (1..5).each do |number|
2    next if number % 2 == 0
3    puts number
4  end
```

```
1
3
5
```

The example demonstrates skipping even numbers within the loop. When the condition number % 2 == 0 is true, the next command is executed, causing the loop to skip the current iteration and move on to the next number.

redo: The redo keyword instructs Ruby to repeat the current iteration of the loop from the beginning, without re-evaluating the loop's condition or fetching the next element in a series. This can be useful for re-processing an element in response to a specific condition.

An example usage of redo is as follows:

```
1  attempts = 0
2  begin
3    puts "Trying to perform an operation"
4    raise "error" if attempts < 2
5  rescue
6    attempts += 1
7    redo
8  end
```

This snippet simulates retrying an operation up to three times in the event of a failure. The redo keyword causes the block to be executed again, allowing for another attempt at the operation.

Ruby's break, next, and redo keywords offer fine-grained control over loop execution. These controls enable developers to construct loops that can dynamically respond to runtime conditions, making them invaluable tools for creating robust and flexible Ruby applications.

3.5 Iterating with for and each

In Ruby programming, iteration is a fundamental concept allowing for the execution of a block of code a specified number of times. Two primary methods for iteration in Ruby are the for loop and the each method. Both serve similar purposes but differ in their implementation and usage within the Ruby environment.

The For Loop

The for loop in Ruby is utilized to iterate over a range or a collection such as an array or a hash. Its syntax is straightforward and resembles iteration constructs in other programming languages. However, it is less commonly used in Ruby due to the presence of more idiomatic options provided by the language, such as the each method.

A basic example of a for loop iterating over a range is as follows:

```
1  for i in 1..5 do
2    puts i
3  end
```

This loop will print the numbers from 1 to 5 inclusively. The range is specified by 1..5, and each value within this range is temporarily assigned to the variable i during each iteration of the loop.

When iterating over arrays using a for loop, the syntax remains largely the same, with the range replaced by the array:

```
1  numbers = [1, 2, 3, 4, 5]
2  for number in numbers do
3    puts number
4  end
```

This example will output each number in the numbers array. Despite its clarity, the for loop is not the preferred method for iteration in Ruby due to its explicit nature and the external iteration pattern it represents.

The Each Method

Ruby's each method represents a more Ruby-esque approach to iteration, fostering internal iteration patterns where the method call itself controls the iteration process. This approach not only simplifies the syntax but also enhances readability and follows the Ruby philosophy of "Convention Over Configuration" more closely.

The each method can be employed on arrays in the following manner:

```
1  numbers = [1, 2, 3, 4, 5]
2  numbers.each do |number|
3    puts number
4  end
```

In this snippet, the block of code within the do...end construct is executed for each element in the numbers array. The current element is passed into the block and assigned to the block variable number, which can then be used within the block.

The each method is not limited to arrays; it also applies to hashes, allowing both the key and the value to be passed into the block:

```
1  capitals = { "USA" => "Washington, D.C.", "France" => "Paris", "Italy" => "Rome"
        }
2  capitals.each do |country, capital|
3    puts "#{capital} is the capital of #{country}"
4  end
```

This example iterates over the capitals hash, printing a statement about each capital and its corresponding country. Here, the each

68

method illustrates its versatility and power in handling collections of various types, embodying the principle of yielding to a block to achieve concise and expressive code.

Comparison and Use Cases

While both the for loop and the each method are capable of iterating over collections, the each method is favored in Ruby due to its encapsulation and adherence to object-oriented principles. The for loop, though occasionally useful for quick scripts or ported code, generally finds less utility in idiomatic Ruby codebases.

Adopting the each method for iteration tasks not only aligns with Ruby's design philosophy but also leads to cleaner, more maintainable code. Ruby developers are encouraged to leverage the each method and appreciate the elegance it brings to the iteration processes.

3.6 Using Iterators: times, upto, downto, and step

Ruby provides several methods for iteration, which significantly simplifies the process of executing a block of code multiple times. These iterators, namely times, upto, downto, and step, offer a concise syntax for loops, reducing the amount of boilerplate code required for common iterative tasks. This section explores each of these iterators in detail, illustrating how they can be adeptly harnessed to perform repetitive operations with elegance.

times Iterator

The times method is a straightforward way to execute a block of code a specified number of times. The syntax is simple: the integer which calls the times method represents the number of iterations,

and the block of code to be executed is provided within curly braces
or do . . . end.

```
1  5.times do |i|
2    puts "Iteration \#\{i+1\}"
3  end
```

The above code outputs:

```
Iteration #1
Iteration #2
Iteration #3
Iteration #4
Iteration #5
```

In this example, i represents the index of the current iteration, starting from 0. This index is optional; omitting it is perfectly valid when
the index is not needed within the block.

upto and downto Iterators

The upto and downto methods facilitate iteration from a starting integer up to or down to another integer, respectively. They provide an
intuitive way to iterate through a range of numbers.

```
1  3.upto(5) do |i|
2    puts "Counting up: \#\{i\}"
3  end
4
5  5.downto(3) do |i|
6    puts "Counting down: \#\{i\}"
7  end
```

This produces:

```
Counting up: 3
Counting up: 4
Counting up: 5
Counting down: 5
Counting down: 4
Counting down: 3
```

Both upto and downto are highly readable, making code that utilizes
them easy to understand at a glance.

step Iterator

The step method is used to iterate over a range of numbers with a specified step size. It is called on an initial value, takes an end value and a step value as arguments, and executes the block for each value in the sequence.

```
1  1.step(10, 2) do |i|
2    puts "Stepping by 2: \#\{i\}"
3  end
```

The output of this code snippet is:

```
Stepping by 2: 1
Stepping by 2: 3
Stepping by 2: 5
Stepping by 2: 7
Stepping by 2: 9
```

1.step(10, 2) iterates from 1 to 10, inclusive, with steps of 2. The step method is versatile, suitable for situations where neither times, upto, nor downto would be as efficient or clear.

The iterators times, upto, downto, and step provide Ruby programmers with powerful tools for repetitive tasks. Whether the requirement is to repeat an operation a fixed number of times, iterate through a range of numbers, or step through a sequence at a specified interval, these iterators offer simple, expressive syntaxes that enhance the readability and maintainability of Ruby code.

3.7 Ranges as Sequences, Conditions, or Intervals

Ruby's range objects offer a versatile way to represent sequences, conditions, or intervals. A range is defined by specifying a start and an end, denoted by two dots (inclusive) or three dots (exclusive). This simple yet powerful tool allows developers to generate sequences of numbers or characters, specify conditions within loops, or define intervals for case statements.

Creating Ranges

Ranges can be created using either two dots (..) to include the end value, or three dots (...) to exclude the end value from the range. Here is how you can define ranges:

```
1   inclusive_range = 1..5 # Includes 1, 2, 3, 4, 5
2   exclusive_range = 1...5 # Includes 1, 2, 3, 4
3   character_range = 'a'..'d' # Includes 'a', 'b', 'c', 'd'
```

Using Ranges as Sequences

Ranges are often used to create sequences of values which can be iterated over. The each method, combined with a block, is a common way to iterate over a range:

```
1   (1..5).each do |number|
2     puts number
3   end
```

The code block above will print numbers from 1 to 5, demonstrating how a range acts as a sequence.

Ranges as Conditions in Loops

Ranges are also useful as conditional expressions within loops. For instance, when checking if a variable falls within a certain interval:

```
1   number = 3
2   puts "Within range" if (1..5) === number
```

The === operator checks if the specified number lies within the given range, printing "Within range" if the condition is true.

Ranges in Case Statements

In Ruby, ranges can be particularly handy in case expressions, allowing for elegant handling of multiple conditions:

```
1  age = 23
2  case age
3  when 0..12
4    puts "Child"
5  when 13..19
6    puts "Teen"
7  else
8    puts "Adult"
9  end
```

This example uses ranges to define intervals for age categories, resulting in a clear and readable case statement.

Conversion to Arrays

Another feature of ranges is their ability to be converted into arrays using the to_a method. This can be useful when a sequence of values is needed as an array:

```
1  number_array = (1..5).to_a # Results in [1, 2, 3, 4, 5]
```

This operation transforms the range into an array containing all the integers from 1 to 5, inclusive.

In summary, Ruby ranges are versatile objects that can represent sequences, conditions, or intervals in a straightforward manner. Their simplicity in syntax and broad applicability in loops, conditional statements, and as sequences make them an indispensable tool in Ruby programming.

3.8   The Enumerable Module: each, map, select, and more

The Enumerable module in Ruby enriches collections, such as arrays and hashes, with a variety of traversal, searching, and sorting methods. This module leverages the capability of collections to enumerate their elements, hence enabling programmers to apply concise, expressive operations on sets of data. Several key methods provided by the Enumerable module, including each, map, select, and others, stand out for their utility and frequency of use in Ruby programming.

each **Method**

The each method serves as the foundation of iteration in Ruby collections. It passes every element of a collection to a given block, allowing for operations to be performed on each element.

```
1  [1, 2, 3].each { |number| puts number * 2 }
```

```
2
4
6
```

In this example, the each method iterates over an array of numbers, multiplying each by two and outputting the result. This method does not alter the original array and returns the original array itself after completion of the iteration.

map **Method**

The map method, also known as collect, applies a given block of code to each element of a collection and returns a new array with the results. This method is particularly useful for transforming elements in a collection.

```
1  result = [1, 2, 3].map { |number| number * 2 }
2  puts result.inspect
```

```
[2, 4, 6]
```

Here, the map method multiplies every element in the array by two, creating a new array with these values. Unlike each, map returns a new array based on the results of the block execution.

select Method

The select method filters a collection based on the truthiness of the block's return value for each element. It returns a new collection containing all elements for which the given block returns a true value.

```
1  evens = [1, 2, 3, 4, 5].select { |number| number.even? }
2  puts evens.inspect
```

```
[2, 4]
```

This example demonstrates filtering an array to include only even numbers using the select method. Similar to map, select generates a new array without modifying the original.

More Enumerable Methods

Beyond each, map, and select, the Enumerable module offers a plethora of methods, including reject, find, reduce, among others, each serving a unique purpose.

- reject is the inverse of select, returning a new array containing elements for which the block returns false or nil.

- find (or detect) searches for and returns the first element for which the block returns true.

- reduce (or inject) accumulates a result across the elements of a collection based on the operations defined within the block.

The Enumerable module significantly contributes to Ruby's expressiveness and efficiency in handling collections. By understanding and utilizing the methods it provides, developers can implement complex operations on collections with succinct, readable code, thereby elevating the quality and maintainability of their Ruby programs.

3.9   Looping with Iterators: each_with_index, map_with_index

Looping plays a critical role in iterating over collections in Ruby, such as arrays or hashes. Ruby enriches the conventional loop constructs with powerful iterators that not only simplify code but also enhance readability and maintainability. Among these, the iterators each_with_index and map_with_index are particularly valuable for situations where the index of the elements being iterated is as important as the element values themselves.

Understanding each_with_index

The each_with_index method combines the functionality of each iterator with the utility of maintaining the current index of the element being processed. This method is ideal for scenarios where both the element and its position within the collection are required for the operation being performed.

A basic syntax of each_with_index is as follows:

```
1  collection.each_with_index do |element, index|
2    # operation using element and index
3  end
```

Here, the collection could be any enumerable object, and the block receives two parameters: the element being iterated over and its index in the collection.

Consider a practical example where we need to print each element of an array alongside its index:

```
1  fruits = ["apple", "banana", "cherry"]
2  fruits.each_with_index do |fruit, index|
3    puts "#{index}: #{fruit}"
4  end
```

The output of this code snippet would be:

```
0: apple
1: banana
2: cherry
```

76

Exploring map_with_index

While each_with_index is great for executing operations that do not necessarily transform the collection, map_with_index comes into play when a new array is needed based on performing operations that involve both elements and their indexes. Unfortunately, map_with_index is not a native Ruby method; however, we can achieve its functionality by combining map.with_index.

This method applies a block to every element of the collection and collects the results into a new array. The block receives the current element and its index as parameters.

To understand map_with_index better, suppose we want to prepend the index of each element before the element itself in a new array:

```
1  fruits = ["apple", "banana", "cherry"]
2  indexed_fruits = fruits.map.with_index do |fruit, index|
3    "#{index}: #{fruit}"
4  end
5
6  puts indexed_fruits
```

Executing the above code will yield the following array as output:

```
["0: apple", "1: banana", "2: cherry"]
```

This example highlights how combining map with with_index can efficiently produce a new array based on the elements and their indices from an existing collection.

each_with_index and map_with_index (via map.with_index) are indispensable Ruby iterators for operations that require access to both the elements of a collection and their indices. Their use promotes cleaner, more maintainable code by abstracting the explicit indexing logic typically required in these scenarios.

Chapter 4

Collection Types: Arrays, Hashes, and Symbols

This chapter examines the core collection types in Ruby: arrays, hashes, and symbols, each serving as fundamental building blocks for organizing and manipulating data. Arrays allow for ordered collections of elements, while hashes enable storage of key-value pairs for quick access and retrieval. Symbols, often used as efficient keys in hashes, provide performance benefits and serve specific use cases in Ruby programs. Through exploring these types, readers will gain insights into effectively managing collections of data in Ruby, leveraging these constructs for more efficient and expressive code.

4.1 Introduction to Collection Types

In Ruby, collection types are pivotal constructs that empower developers to organize, manage, and manipulate data with remarkable efficiency and expressiveness. There are three primary collection types that form the backbone of data structure manipulation in Ruby: arrays, hashes, and symbols. Each type serves a distinct purpose, enabling a wide range of data organization strategies that cater to the nuanced needs of different programming scenarios.

Arrays in Ruby are ordered collections of elements, where each element can be accessed by its index. They are incredibly versatile, allowing for a broad spectrum of operations including adding, removing, and traversing elements. Arrays are ideal for situations where maintaining the sequence of the data is crucial.

```
1  # Example: Creating and manipulating an array
2  numbers = [1, 2, 3, 4, 5]
3  numbers.push(6) # Adding an element to the end
4  puts numbers.inspect # Output: [1, 2, 3, 4, 5, 6]
```

Hashes, on the other hand, are an implementation of a data structure known as a dictionary or a map, which stores key-value pairs. Keys are unique identifiers that map to corresponding values, making hashes exceptionally efficient for lookup operations where retrieving a value based on its key is a common task.

```
1  # Example: Creating and accessing a hash
2  person = { "name" => "Alice", "age" => 30 }
3  puts person["name"] # Output: Alice
```

Symbols in Ruby represent names and some strings inside a Ruby program. They are unique, immutable, and reusable, making them excellent choices for identifiers, particularly as keys in hashes. Unlike strings, symbols of the same name are initialized and exist in memory only once, offering performance benefits, especially in scenarios involving frequent access by key.

```
1  # Example: Using symbols as hash keys
2  person = { :name => "Alice", :age => 30 }
3  puts person[:name] # Output: Alice
```

Understanding and effectively utilizing these collection types are fundamental for Ruby programmers.   Arrays and hashes are versatile tools for creating structured data sets, while symbols offer a means of defining and accessing data with efficiency and clarity. Throughout this chapter, the focus will be on diving deep into each of these collection types, exploring their creation, access patterns, manipulation techniques, and their use in organizing complex data structures. Additionally, we will look into the Ruby Enumerable module, which provides a powerful set of methods for searching, sorting, filtering, and performing other operations on collections. The knowledge gained from this chapter will serve as a solid foundation for writing more efficient and maintainable Ruby code.

```
Output for the symbol hash key example:
Alice
```

4.2 Arrays in Ruby: Creation, Access, and Manipulation

Arrays in Ruby are ordered, integer-indexed collections of any object. Arrays allow you to store a collection of items in a single variable, making it a versatile and essential tool for data organization and manipulation in Ruby programming. This section covers how to create, access, and manipulate arrays in Ruby, providing the foundation for working with collections.

Creating Arrays

There are several ways to create arrays in Ruby. The most direct method is to use the array literal notation, which involves enclosing items within square brackets, separated by commas. For example:

```
1  numbers = [1, 2, 3, 4, 5]
2  words = ['hello', 'world']
3  mixed = [1, 'two', 3.0, :four]
```

Another method to create arrays is by using the Array.new method, which can initialize arrays in various ways:

- Without arguments, creates an empty array: `empty_array = Array.new`.

- With an integer argument, creates an array with that number of nil elements: `nil_array = Array.new(3)`.

- With an integer and an object as arguments, creates an array with the object repeated: `default_array = Array.new(3, 'default')`.

Accessing Array Elements

Elements in an array are accessed using their index, which starts at 0 for the first element. Use square brackets and the index to access an element:

```
1  fruits = ['apple', 'banana', 'cherry']
2  puts fruits[0] # Output: apple
3  puts fruits[2] # Output: cherry
```

Ruby also supports negative indices, starting from -1 for the last element, -2 for the second to last, and so on:

```
1  puts fruits[-1] # Output: cherry
```

Manipulating Arrays

Arrays in Ruby can be manipulated in several ways, including adding, removing, and modifying elements.

Adding Elements

Elements can be added to arrays using the << operator or the push method:

```
1  fruits << 'date'
2  fruits.push('elderberry')
```

Removing Elements

Elements can be removed using the pop and shift methods. pop removes the last element, while shift removes the first:

```
1   fruits.pop # Removes 'elderberry'
2   fruits.shift # Removes 'apple'
```

Modifying Elements

Elements in an array can be modified by assigning a new value to a specific index:

```
1   fruits[0] = 'apricot'
```

This section provided an overview of how to create, access, and manipulate arrays in Ruby. Arrays are a versatile tool in Ruby, allowing you to store and manipulate collections of data effectively. Understanding how to work with arrays is fundamental to performing more complex data organization and manipulation tasks in Ruby.

4.3 Hashes in Ruby: Creation, Access, and Manipulation

In this section, we will discuss the intricacies of working with hashes in Ruby. Hashes, also referred to as associative arrays, dictionaries, or maps in other programming languages, enable the storage and management of data pairs. Each entry in a hash consists of a unique key and a corresponding value, facilitating O(1) access complexity for searching and retrieval.

Creating Hashes

To initialize a hash in Ruby, several methods can be employed. The most straightforward approach is to use curly braces {}, inside which key-value pairs are separated by commas, with the key and value of each pair separated by a hash rocket => or a colon : when symbols are used as keys.

```
1   empty_hash = {}
```

83

```
2 | hash_with_string_keys = {'name' => 'Alice', 'age' => 30}
3 | hash_with_symbol_keys = {name: 'Bob', age: 25}
```

Another method to create hashes is by using the Hash.new method, which allows the setting of a default value for keys that do not exist in the hash.

```
1 | hash_with_default = Hash.new(0) # 0 is the default value
```

Accessing Values

The value associated with a key can be retrieved by placing the key inside square brackets [] following the hash name.

```
1 | puts hash_with_string_keys['name'] # Output: Alice
2 | puts hash_with_symbol_keys[:age] # Output: 25
```

If a key does not exist, nil is returned, or the default value if one was set during the hash initialization.

Manipulating Hashes

Adding a new key-value pair to an existing hash is straightforward; simply assign a value to a key using the square bracket notation.

```
1 | hash_with_string_keys['height'] = 170
```

To delete a key-value pair, use the delete method, passing the key as the argument.

```
1 | hash_with_string_keys.delete('age')
```

Ruby provides several methods for iterating over hashes, allowing for the execution of code blocks on each key-value pair. The each method, for example, can be used as follows:

```
1 | hash_with_symbol_keys.each do |key, value|
2 |   puts "#{key}: #{value}"
3 | end
```

This will output each key-value pair in the console. Other useful iteration methods include each_key, each_value, and each_pair, the latter being synonymous with each.

Merging Hashes

Hashes can be merged using the merge method, which takes another hash as an argument and returns a new hash containing the contents of both. If there are duplicate keys, the values from the hash being merged will overwrite those in the original hash.

```
1  merged_hash = hash_with_string_keys.merge(hash_with_symbol_keys)
```

It is essential to note that merge does not modify the original hashes; instead, it returns a new hash. To mutate the caller, use merge!.

This section has covered the creation, access, and manipulation of hashes in Ruby. Understanding these operations is pivotal for managing key-value paired data efficiently.

4.4 Symbols: Understanding Their Use and Performance Benefits

Symbols in Ruby hold a unique place among the collection types due to their immutable nature and efficient way of representation internally within the Ruby interpreter. A symbol, indicated by a colon (:) followed by a name, is essentially a string that cannot be altered. Unlike strings, which can be modified and occupy new memory space with each change, a symbol remains constant, with a single instance in memory for each unique symbol name. This distinction offers various performance benefits and use cases within Ruby programs, particularly when employed as keys in hashes or for identifying method names and other identifiers.

To illustrate the creation of symbols, consider the following example:

```
1  :username
2  :password
```

```
3  :"multiple_words_symbol"
```

Each of these lines defines a symbol. The first two examples show simple symbol creation, while the third example demonstrates how symbols can encompass multiple words if encapsulated in quotes. It is important to note that, despite their appearance, symbols and strings are not interchangeable. For instance, :username and "username" represent a symbol and a string, respectively, and they are distinct types of objects within Ruby.

A primary use of symbols in Ruby is as keys in hashes. Owing to their immutable nature, symbols provide consistency and efficient memory usage when used as hash keys. This is demonstrated in the following code snippet:

```
1  user_info = { :name => "John Doe", :age => 30, :email => "john@example.com" }
```

In this hash, :name, :age, and :email are symbols used as keys. When accessing or manipulating hash elements, using symbols as keys ensures quick lookups and avoids the overhead associated with string keys, which might be created afresh each time they are used, thus occupying more memory.

The performance benefit of symbols is evident in their object id consistency. Every unique symbol in Ruby has a fixed object id, whereas strings, even with identical content, have different object ids if they are distinct instances. This can be demonstrated with the following Ruby code:

```
1  puts :test.object_id == :test.object_id # Output: true
2  puts "test".object_id == "test".object_id # Output: false
```

The above code snippet underscores the single instance nature of symbols as compared to strings, showcasing the efficiency gained, particularly in scenarios that involve frequent lookup or comparison operations.

However, it is incumbent upon the developer to use symbols judiciously. Their immutable and single-instance characteristics, while beneficial in many contexts, also mean that an excessively large number of unique symbols can lead to memory bloat since symbols are not garbage collected in the same way as strings or other objects. This potential pitfall underscores the importance of leveraging symbols primarily in situations where their unique benefits are most impactful, such as hash keys, identifiers, or fixed labels within a program's logic.

Understanding the use and performance benefits of symbols is pivotal for Ruby developers aiming to write efficient and effective code. By employing symbols judiciously, particularly in hashes or as consistent identifiers, developers can leverage Ruby's design to achieve more performant and expressive code constructs.

4.5   Working with Nested Collections

Nested collections in Ruby are a powerful mechanism to store and manage data structured in a hierarchical manner. This capability is critically important in a wide array of programming scenarios, from processing JSON data returned by web services to managing complex data relationships within applications. Understanding how to efficiently work with nested arrays and hashes is vital for Ruby programmers aiming to implement sophisticated data structures.

Nested Arrays

A nested array is an array that contains other arrays as elements. This structure can be visualized as a matrix or a table, where each element of the parent array can be an array representing a row of data.

Consider the following example:

```
1  matrix = [
2    [1, 2, 3],
3    [4, 5, 6],
4    [7, 8, 9]
5  ]
```

To access an element in a nested array, you need to specify two indices: the first for the position within the outer array, and the second for the position within the inner array. For example, to retrieve the number 5 from the `matrix` array:

```
element = matrix[1][1]
puts element
```

```
5
```

Nested Hashes

Nested hashes, where a hash contains other hashes or arrays as values, are commonly used to represent more complex data structures. This is particularly evident when working with data in formats such as JSON, which naturally maps to nested hash structures in Ruby.

Here is an example of a nested hash:

```
person = {
  name: "John Doe",
  address: {
    street: "123 Ruby Lane",
    city: "Ruby City",
    zip: "12345"
  },
  hobbies: ["coding", "reading", "cycling"]
}
```

To access values in a nested hash, chain the keys together until you reach the desired data. For instance, to access the city name from the person hash:

```
city = person[:address][:city]
puts city
```

```
Ruby City
```

Manipulating Nested Collections

Manipulating data within nested collections involves iterating over elements using loops or enumerable methods and, possibly, modifying them. Ruby's enumerable methods, such as `each`, `map`, and `select`, can be particularly useful.

For example, to increase each number by 1 in a nested array:

```
incremented_matrix = matrix.map do |row|
  row.map do |element|
    element + 1
  end
end

puts incremented_matrix.inspect
```

```
[[2, 3, 4], [5, 6, 7], [8, 9, 10]]
```

When working with nested structures, it is crucial to be mindful of the level at which operations are performed, ensuring that methods are applied at the correct depth to achieve the desired outcome.

Working with nested collections is a fundamental aspect of Ruby programming, enabling developers to build and manipulate complex data structures efficiently. Mastery of nested arrays and hashes, coupled with Ruby's powerful enumerable methods, allows for the creation of expressive and efficient code. Through practice and exploration of various use cases, developers can deepen their understanding of nested collections and their applications in Ruby programming.

4.6 Common Enumerable Methods for Arrays and Hashes

In this section, we will discuss the Enumerable module, a central element in Ruby's collection manipulation toolkit. The Enumerable module equips both arrays and hashes with a comprehensive set of methods for searching, sorting, filtering, and aggregating data. To understand the power and flexibility of these methods, we will explore specific examples involving both arrays and hashes.

The each Method

```
1  [1, 2, 3].each do |number|
2    puts number
3  end
```

```
1
2
3
```

The each method iterates over each element in an array or each key-value pair in a hash, allowing for operations to be performed on each element or pair. Notice that this method does not alter the original collection but rather serves as a foundation for other enumerable methods.

Selecting Elements with select

```
1  numbers = [1, 2, 3, 4, 5]
2  even_numbers = numbers.select { |number| number.even? }
3  puts even_numbers
```

```
[2, 4]
```

The select method filters a collection based on a specified condition. In this example, select is used to find all even numbers in an array. Similarly, it can be used on hashes to filter key-value pairs according to the condition provided in the block.

Transforming Elements with map

```
1  numbers = [1, 2, 3, 4, 5]
2  squared_numbers = numbers.map { |number| number ** 2 }
3  puts squared_numbers
```

```
[1, 4, 9, 16, 25]
```

The map method, also known as collect, applies a given block of code to each element of the collection, returning a new array with the transformed elements. It is particularly useful for operations that require each element to be manipulated or adjusted in some way.

Finding an Element with `find`

```
1  numbers = [1, 2, 3, 4, 5]
2  first_even_number = numbers.find { |number| number.even? }
3  puts first_even_number
```

2

The `find` method returns the first element for which the block returns `true`. This method is useful for quickly locating an element in a large collection without having to manually search for it. If no element is found that satisfies the condition, `find` returns `nil`.

Aggregating Values with `reduce`

```
1  numbers = [1, 2, 3, 4, 5]
2  sum = numbers.reduce(0) { |acc, number| acc + number }
3  puts sum
```

15

The `reduce` method, sometimes known as `inject`, combines all elements of the collection by applying a binary operation, specified by a block. In the example above, `reduce` is used to find the sum of all numbers in the array by starting with an initial value of 0 and then adding each element to the accumulator variable `acc`.

The flexibility of the Enumerable module makes it a powerful tool for working with collections in Ruby. By mastering these methods, developers can write more expressive, efficient, and elegant code for manipulating arrays and hashes.

4.7 Sorting and Filtering Collections

Sorting and filtering are critical operations when working with data collections, allowing not only for organization but also for efficient

91

data retrieval and manipulation. In Ruby, arrays and hashes offer built-in methods to facilitate these operations, making it straightforward to manage collections.

Sorting Arrays: The sort and sort_by methods are integral for ordering array elements. The sort method is utilized for arrays containing elements of the same type, applying a default ascending order. However, when specific sorting criteria are required, or the array contains complex objects such as hashes, sort_by becomes invaluable.

```
1  numbers = [5, 3, 8, 6, 1]
2  sorted_numbers = numbers.sort
```

In the code snippet above, sorted_numbers will yield:

```
[1, 3, 5, 6, 8]
```

To customize sorting, a block can be provided to sort or sort_by, dictating the sorting logic.

```
1  words = ['banana', 'apple', 'pear', 'orange']
2  sorted_words = words.sort_by { |word| word.length }
```

This example sorts the words by their length, resulting in:

```
["pear", "apple", "banana", "orange"]
```

Filtering Arrays: Ruby arrays incorporate the select method for filtering, enabling the extraction of elements that meet specific criteria. The method evaluates each element against the provided block and includes it in the result if the block returns true.

```
1  numbers = [1, 2, 3, 4, 5]
2  even_numbers = numbers.select { |number| number.even? }
```

By executing the above code, even_numbers is assigned:

```
[2, 4]
```

Sorting Hashes: Similar to arrays, Ruby hashes can be sorted by keys or values using sort or sort_by. Given that sort on a hash returns an array of arrays, each containing a key-value pair, additional steps may be required to maintain a hash's structure when sorting by values.

```
1  fruit_quantities = {banana: 5, apple: 2, pear: 3}
2  sorted_by_quantity = fruit_quantities.sort_by { |fruit, quantity| quantity }
```

This produces an array of tuples sorted by the fruit quantities:

```
[[:apple, 2], [:pear, 3], [:banana, 5]]
```

Filtering Hashes: The select method is equally useful for hashes, allowing for the selection of key-value pairs that satisfy a specific condition.

```
1  fruit_quantities = {banana: 5, apple: 2, pear: 3}
2  high_quantity = fruit_quantities.select { |fruit, quantity| quantity > 3 }
```

The resulting hash, high_quantity, contains:

```
{:banana=>5}
```

In summary, Ruby's built-in methods for sorting and filtering collections simplify the manipulation of arrays and hashes, contributing to more readable, efficient, and expressive code. Whether working with simple or complex collections, these operations are fundamental for data organization and retrieval in Ruby programming.

4.8 Converting Between Arrays and Hashes

Converting between arrays and hashes is a common task in Ruby programming, allowing developers to leverage the strengths of each collection type as needed. This versatility enhances code expressiveness and efficiency. The following sections describe methods and practices for converting between arrays and hashes.

From Arrays to Hashes

Conversion from an array to a hash can be achieved through several methods, depending on the array's structure. A common scenario involves converting an array of pairs into a hash, where each pair comprises two elements: a key and a value.

```
1  pairs = [[:name, "John"], [:age, 30], [:city, "New York"]]
2  hash = pairs.to_h
```

The to_h method transforms the array of pairs into a hash, assigning the first element of each pair as the key and the second as the value. The output is shown below:

```
{:name=>"John", :age=>30, :city=>"New York"}
```

In cases where the array is flat (e.g., [key1, value1, key2, value2]), the array should first be converted into an array of pairs before applying the to_h method. This can be accomplished with the each_slice method from the Enumerable module:

```
1  flat_array = [:name, "John", :age, 30, :city, "New York"]
2  pairs = flat_array.each_slice(2).to_a
3  hash = pairs.to_h
```

From Hashes to Arrays

Converting a hash back into an array is straightforward and can be accomplished in various ways, depending on the desired array structure. To convert a hash into an array of pairs (where each pair is an array consisting of a key and a value), the to_a method is used:

```
1  hash = {name: "John", age: 30, city: "New York"}
2  pairs_array = hash.to_a
```

The resulting array is as follows:

```
[[:name, "John"], [:age, 30], [:city, "New York"]]
```

For scenarios requiring separate arrays of keys and values, the keys and values methods can be employed:

```
1   keys = hash.keys
2   values = hash.values
```

These methods produce the following arrays:

```
[:name, :age, :city]
["John", 30, "New York"]
```

Practical Applications

Understanding how to convert between arrays and hashes is essential for data manipulation tasks, such as processing CSV files, API responses, or database query results. Mastery of these conversions enhances a developer's ability to choose the most appropriate data structure for a given task, streamlining code and improving performance.

When working with data retrieved from external sources, it often arrives in a format that is not immediately suitable for the intended processing task. For example, CSV data might be parsed into arrays, but a hash representation could be more convenient for accessing specific elements. Conversely, when preparing data for output or serialization, converting a complex hash to an array of simpler elements might be more practical.

By employing the methods and techniques outlined in this section, developers can efficiently navigate between these versatile collection types, adapting the data structure to fit the requirements of their code rather than contorting their logic to accommodate suboptimal data representations.

4.9   Using Symbols as Hash Keys

In Ruby, symbols are commonly used as hash keys for several reasons: their immutability, memory efficiency, and faster key lookup compared to using strings. This section will illustrate how to use symbols as keys in hashes and delve into the advantages they offer.

Defining Hashes with Symbol Keys

To define a hash using symbols as keys, you can use the following syntax:

```
1  student_ages = {:Lisa => 24, :John => 22, :Sam => 19}
```

Alternatively, Ruby offers a more modern and concise syntax for symbol keys:

```
1  student_ages = {Lisa: 24, John: 22, Sam: 19}
```

In this notation, Ruby automatically understands that the keys are symbols, simplifying the syntax and improving readability. This is the preferred style for hashes with symbol keys in Ruby.

Accessing Values Using Symbol Keys

To access the value associated with a symbol key in a hash, use the key inside brackets following the hash name:

```
1  puts student_ages[:Lisa] # Output: 24
```

This code retrieves the age of Lisa from the student_ages hash using the symbol :Lisa as the key.

Advantages of Using Symbols as Keys

Using symbols as keys in hashes provides several benefits:

- **Memory Efficiency:** Symbols are stored in memory only once, no matter how many times they are used. In contrast, every instance of a string is stored separately, even if two strings contain the exact same characters. This makes symbols a more memory-efficient option for keys.

- **Immutability:** Unlike strings, which can be modified, symbols are immutable. This means their value remains constant, which is a desirable property for hash keys to ensure consistent access to values.

- **Faster Key Lookups:** Since symbols are immutable and uniquely stored, Ruby can perform faster key lookups for symbols compared to strings. This can lead to performance improvements, especially in larger hashes or applications where hash lookups are frequent.

Converting Strings to Symbols

There may be scenarios where you need to convert strings to symbols, particularly when working with dynamic keys. Ruby makes this conversion straightforward:

```
1  dynamic_key = "user_name".to_sym
2  user_info = {user_name: "johndoe"}
3
4  puts user_info[dynamic_key] # Output: johndoe
```

In this code snippet, the string "user_name" is converted to a symbol using the to_sym method, which allows it to be used as a key to access values in the user_info hash.

Utilizing symbols as keys in hashes offers significant advantages in Ruby, including improved memory efficiency, immutability, and faster lookup times. By adopting symbols for hash keys, developers can write more performant and robust Ruby code. When given the choice between symbols and strings for hash keys, symbols are generally the preferred approach for the reasons outlined in this section.

4.10   Set: Another Useful Collection Type

The Ruby language encompasses several collection types, with arrays and hashes being the most pervasive. However, another type worth discussing is the Set. Differing fundamentally from arrays and hashes, a Set is a collection that is unordered and ensures that all its elements are unique. This means no two elements in a Set can be the same, a property that can be particularly useful in scenarios where the uniqueness of elements is paramount. To utilize Set in Ruby, it is necessary to require the Set library as it is not part of the Ruby language's core library.

To commence using Set, the first step involves requiring the Set library in the Ruby script as follows:

```
1   require 'set'
```

Once the library is included, a new Set can be created either by direct instantiation or by converting an array to a Set. Below are examples illustrating both methods:

```
1   # Direct instantiation
2   numbers = Set.new([1, 2, 3, 4, 5])
3
4   # Converting an array to a set
5   array = [1, 2, 2, 3, 4, 4, 5]
6   numbers_set = array.to_set
```

In the second example, the array is converted to a Set, which automatically removes any duplicate elements, illustrating one of the Set's primary benefits: ensuring element uniqueness.

Operations on a Set include adding and deleting elements, much like arrays. However, since a Set maintains unique elements, adding an element that already exists in the Set has no effect:

```
1   numbers.add(6) # Adds element '6' to the set
2   numbers.add(3) # No effect, as '3' already exists in the set
3   numbers.delete(1) # Removes element '1' from the set
```

Importantly, a Set does not maintain elements in any specific order. Therefore, operations that rely on the order of elements, such as indexing, are not supported.

Set operations also encompass those for union, intersection, and difference, which can be invaluable when dealing with multiple collections:

```
1  set1 = Set.new([1, 2, 3])
2  set2 = Set.new([3, 4, 5])
3
4  union = set1 | set2 # Union: [1, 2, 3, 4, 5]
5  intersection = set1 & set2 # Intersection: [3]
6  difference = set1 - set2 # Difference: [1, 2]
```

Each operation produces a new Set, with the | operator combining all elements from both sets (while removing duplicates), the & operator identifying common elements between the two sets, and the - operator removing elements found in the second set from the first.

Set is a powerful collection type that offers performance benefits, particularly in operations that require checking the presence of an element, which is faster in a Set compared to an array due to the underlying implementation. It is an indispensable tool when the uniqueness of elements is crucial, or when set operations such as union, intersection, and difference are required to solve a problem.

4.11   Best Practices for Working with Collections

Working with collection types in Ruby—arrays, hashes, and symbols—requires adherence to certain best practices to ensure code efficiency, readability, and maintainability. This section delineates several key strategies for optimizing the use and management of collection types in Ruby programming.

- **Prefer Symbols for Hash Keys**: When defining hash keys, symbols are generally more efficient than strings due to their immutability and the internal way Ruby handles them. For example:

```
1  my_hash = { :name => "Alice", :age => 30 }
```

  Symbols as keys enhance performance, especially in scenarios involving large datasets.

- **Utilize Enumerable Methods**: Both arrays and hashes include the Enumerable module, which provides a plethora of methods for traversing, searching, sorting, and filtering collections. Employing these methods can lead to more concise and expressive code. For instance:

```
1  numbers = [1, 2, 3, 4, 5]
2  doubled_numbers = numbers.map { |number| number * 2 }
```

This example uses the .map method to iterate over an array and double each element, demonstrating the power and convenience of Enumerable methods.

- **Avoid Modifying Collections While Iterating**: Altering a collection's size (e.g., adding or removing elements) while iterating over it can lead to unexpected behavior or errors. To prevent this, consider iterating over a duplicate of the collection or accumulate changes to apply post-iteration.

- **Consider Set for Unique Collections**: For cases requiring the storage of unique elements, the Set class should be considered. Set is similar to an array but enforces uniqueness of its elements, which can simplify certain operations and intents. It is particularly useful when the order of elements is not of concern.

- **Use Select and Reject for Filtering**: To filter collections, the select and reject methods offer a more idiomatic way compared to manually constructing loops. For example, to filter out all odd numbers from an array:

```
1  numbers = [1, 2, 3, 4, 5]
2  even_numbers = numbers.select { |number| number.even? }
```

- **Leverage Lazy Evaluation for Large Collections**: Ruby 2.0 introduced Enumerator::Lazy to allow for lazy enumeration of collections. This is especially beneficial for working with large datasets or potentially infinite series, as it helps to significantly reduce memory usage and computational effort by evaluating elements only as needed.

- **Deep Duplication of Nested Collections**: When duplicating collections that contain other collections (e.g., arrays of hashes), ensure that a deep duplicate is performed. This prevents the original and duplicated collections from sharing nested objects, thus avoiding unintended side-effects stemming from mutable state.

Following these best practices can significantly improve the performance and reliability of Ruby programs that make extensive use of collection types. Additionally, adhering to these guidelines will enhance code readability and maintainability, making it easier for other developers to understand and work with your code.

Chapter 5

Methods, Blocks, and Procs

This chapter delves into the mechanisms Ruby provides for grouping and reusing code: methods, blocks, and procs. It covers how to define and invoke methods, utilize blocks for handling code that should be executed within the context of a method, and employ procs and lambdas for storing blocks of code that can be passed around and executed. Understanding these tools is fundamental for writing DRY (Don't Repeat Yourself), manageable, and flexible Ruby code, enabling programmers to encapsulate logic in reusable components and handle variable behavior in a clean, idiomatic way.

5.1   Defining and Invoking Methods

Let's start with the basics of defining methods in Ruby. A method in Ruby is a set of expressions that performs a specific task and can be called or invoked anywhere in your program. Methods are fundamental for organizing code into manageable, reusable blocks.

Defining a method in Ruby begins with the def keyword, followed by the method name. The method body comes next, enclosed within the method definition and the end keyword. Here's the general structure:

```
1  def method_name
2    # method body
3  end
```

Method names should be chosen carefully to clearly express what the method does. Ruby follows a naming convention of using snake_case for method names, which means all letters are lowercase, and spaces are replaced by underscores.

Arguments can be passed to methods to make them more flexible and dynamic. Arguments are specified between parentheses immediately after the method name.

```
1  def greet(name)
2    puts "Hello, #{name}!"
3  end
```

In this example, name is an argument to the greet method, which outputs a greeting to the console.

Invoking or calling a method is done simply by writing its name followed by any necessary arguments within parentheses. If a method does not require any arguments, parentheses can be omitted.

```
1  greet("Alice")
```

This line of code calls the greet method with "Alice" as the argument, resulting in the output:

```
Hello, Alice!
```

It's crucial to understand the concept of return values in the context of method definitions. By default, Ruby methods return the value of the last expression evaluated. However, an explicit return statement can be used to return a value prematurely, overriding the default behavior.

```
1  def add(a, b)
2    return a + b
3  end
```

This add method takes two arguments and returns their sum. Despite Ruby's implicit return, it's sometimes advantageous or necessary to use an explicit return for clarity or control flow.

In summary, defining and invoking methods in Ruby is a straightforward process. Methods enhance the organization, reuse, and readability of code. With a clear understanding of how to effectively define and use methods, arguments, and return values, developers can create more dynamic and flexible Ruby applications.

5.2 Arguments and Parameters: Default, Keyword, and Variable-Length

In this section, we delve into the intricacies of defining methods in Ruby, specifically focusing on how arguments and parameters can be utilized to create flexible and robust methods. Ruby's approach to method arguments facilitates the design of methods that can adapt to various use cases, ranging from methods that require a fixed set of parameters to those that handle an arbitrary number of arguments or leverage named parameters for enhanced clarity.

Default Arguments: Ruby allows the specification of default values for method parameters, enabling methods to be invoked with or without those arguments. This feature is particularly useful for creating methods with optional parameters. Consider the following method definition:

```
1  def greet(name="World")
2    puts "Hello, #{name}!"
3  end
```

In this example, the greet method accepts a single parameter, name, with a default value of "World". This enables the method to be called in two ways:

```
greet("Alice")   # Output: Hello, Alice!
greet            # Output: Hello, World!
```

Keyword Arguments: Introduced in Ruby 2.0, keyword arguments

allow the explicit naming of method parameters when invoking a
method. This not only enhances the readability of the code but also
eliminates the need to remember the order of parameters. A method
utilizing keyword arguments could be defined as follows:

```
1  def describe_vehicle(type:, model:, year:)
2    puts "Vehicle Type: #{type}, Model: #{model}, Year: #{year}"
3  end
```

Invoking the `describe_vehicle` method with keyword arguments
would look like this:

```
describe_vehicle(type: "Sedan", model: "Toyota Camry", year: 2021)
```

Variable-Length Arguments (Splat Operator): To define methods
that accept an arbitrary number of arguments, Ruby employs the
splat operator (*). This feature is invaluable for creating methods
that need to process an undefined number of inputs. An example is
as follows:

```
1  def sum(*numbers)
2    numbers.reduce(0) { |sum, number| sum + number }
3  end
```

When invoked, the sum method can handle any number of arguments,
as demonstrated below:

```
sum(1, 2, 3, 4, 5) # Output: 15
sum(10, 20)        # Output: 30
```

Combining Argument Types: Ruby methods can be designed to include a mix of default, keyword, and variable-length arguments, offering a high degree of flexibility. For instance:

```
1  def create_profile(name, age, *hobbies, country: "Unknown")
2    puts "Name: #{name}, Age: #{age}, Country: #{country}"
3    puts "Hobbies: " + hobbies.join(", ")
4  end
```

In this `create_profile` method, the use of different argument types
showcases Ruby's capability to handle complex method signatures
effectively.

Understanding the nuances of method arguments and parameters in Ruby is crucial for writing clear, flexible, and maintainable code. By leveraging default, keyword, and variable-length arguments, developers can create methods that are both powerful and easy to use.

5.3 Return Values and Return Statements

The concept of return values is integral to understanding how methods communicate results back to the caller. In Ruby, every method call returns a value, even if it is not explicitly stated. By default, a Ruby method returns the value of the last expression evaluated within its body. However, this behavior can be overridden using return statements to explicitly specify the value or values to be returned from a method.

Consider the following code snippet, which defines a simple method that takes two arguments and returns their sum:

```
1  def add_two_numbers(num1, num2)
2    sum = num1 + num2
3    return sum
4  end
```

In this example, the return statement is used to explicitly return the value of the variable sum. However, the return keyword is optional when the value to be returned is the result of the last expression evaluated, as shown in the simplified version below:

```
1  def add_two_numbers(num1, num2)
2    num1 + num2
3  end
```

Both versions of the add_two_numbers method will behave identically, demonstrating that explicit return statements are not always necessary. Yet, there are scenarios where the explicit use of return is advantageous or even required. Consider a method that needs to terminate its execution prematurely based on some condition:

```
1  def check_age(age)
2    return "Invalid age" if age < 0
```

107

```
3    if age < 18
4      "Minor"
5    else
6      "Adult"
7    end
8  end
```

In this example, the `return` statement is used to immediately exit the method and return a specific message if the provided age is less than 0. Without the `return` statement, the method would continue to evaluate the remaining conditions, which could lead to incorrect or unexpected results.

It is also possible for a method to return multiple values by listing them after the `return` statement, separated by commas. Ruby automatically constructs an array containing the specified values. Observe the following example:

```
1  def calculate_statistics(scores)
2    min = scores.min
3    max = scores.max
4    average = scores.sum / scores.length.to_f
5    return min, max, average
6  end
```

Calling this method with an array of scores will return an array containing the minimum score, maximum score, and average score, in that order:

```
min, max, average = calculate_statistics([10, 20, 30, 40, 50])
puts min        # Output: 10
puts max        # Output: 50
puts average    # Output: 30.0
```

When utilizing return statements, especially for returning multiple values, it is crucial to consider the readability and maintainability of the code. Excessive or unnecessary use of return statements can obscure the method's intent and flow, making it harder to follow and understand.

In summary, while Ruby methods automatically return the last expression evaluated, return statements provide the flexibility to control the flow of a method and explicitly specify return values. Whether to use them depends on the specific requirements of the method and the clarity of the code.

5.4 Understanding Blocks: The Basics

Ruby, being a language that encourages flexibility and productivity, offers various ways to write concise and reusable code. Among these, blocks stand out as one of the simplest yet powerful features. A block in Ruby is a chunk of code enclosed either within braces {} or between a do and an end keyword. Blocks can be passed to methods as arguments and are invoked from within the method using the yield keyword.

To grasp the concept of blocks, consider a basic example where a method is designed to execute any code passed to it within a block:

```
1  def demonstrate_block
2    puts "Before the block"
3    yield
4    puts "After the block"
5  end
6
7  demonstrate_block { puts "Inside the block" }
```

When the above script is executed, the method demonstrate_block is called with a block that prints "Inside the block". The output will be:

```
Before the block
Inside the block
After the block
```

This example illustrates the primary role of blocks: they allow you to inject additional code into a method, with the method controlling when the block's code is executed via yield.

Blocks can also receive parameters from the method. If a method contains variables within parentheses next to the yield keyword, these variables are passed to the block. Within the block, these variables are accessible between vertical bars (|). Here is an example:

```
1  def demonstrate_block_with_parameters
2    yield("Hello", 42)
3  end
4
5  demonstrate_block_with_parameters { |string, number| puts "#{string}, the number
       is #{number}" }
```

109

The output of this script would be:

```
Hello, the number is 42
```

In this case, the method `demonstrate_block_with_parameters` calls the provided block with two parameters, which are received inside the block and used in the `puts` statement.

Understanding the difference between the single-line and multi-line block syntax is also crucial. Although they perform identical tasks, the braces syntax is generally used for single-line blocks, while the do-end syntax is preferred for multi-line blocks. This is not a strict rule, but rather a convention followed by the Ruby community for readability purposes:

- Single-line block:

```
1   [1, 2, 3].each { |number| puts number }
```

- Multi-line block:

```
1   [1, 2, 3].each do |number|
2     puts number
3     puts number*2
4   end
```

By understanding blocks, Ruby programmers gain a powerful tool for making their code more flexible and reusable. Blocks can be thought of as anonymous chunks of code that can be inserted at specific points in a method's execution. This capability is fundamental for achieving DRY (Don't Repeat Yourself) code and allows for sophisticated manipulation of data with minimal code.

5.5   Yielding to Blocks Inside Methods

Yielding to blocks inside methods allows Ruby programmers to write flexible and reusable code. When a method yields, it pauses its execution and transfers control to the block provided at the method call. This technique is especially useful for customizing the behavior of a method based on the needs of the caller, without altering the method's code.

To illustrate this concept, consider the following example:

```
1  def greeting
2    puts "Good morning!"
3    yield
4    puts "Good night!"
5  end
6
7  greeting { puts "How are you today?" }
```

In the example above, the greeting method outputs "Good morning!" to the console, then yields to the block passed during its invocation, which outputs "How are you today?", and finally, after the block has been executed, the method resumes and outputs "Good night!".

```
Good morning!
How are you today?
Good night!
```

The ability to yield to a block allows methods to execute code blocks that can vary at each method call, making the methods highly versatile. For scenarios where the method caller might not provide a block, Ruby provides the block_given? method, which returns true if a block is provided and false otherwise. This can prevent potential errors from calling yield without an associated block. Here is an example:

```
1  def conditional_greeting
2    puts "Hello, everyone!"
3    if block_given?
4      yield
5    else
6      puts "No personal greeting provided."
7    end
8  end
9
10 conditional_greeting
11 conditional_greeting { puts "It's a pleasure to meet you!" }
```

This approach allows the conditional_greeting method to check for the presence of a block. If a block is provided, it yields to that

111

block; otherwise, it proceeds with a default action, ensuring the method functions correctly in both cases.

```
Hello, everyone!
No personal greeting provided.
Hello, everyone!
It's a pleasure to meet you!
```

Another aspect of yielding to blocks is passing arguments to the block from within the method. Methods can provide values to the block by passing them as arguments to the `yield` statement, which can then be used inside the block. For instance:

```
1  def user_info(name)
2    puts "Collecting information for #{name}:"
3    yield(name, 25) if block_given?
4  end
5
6  user_info("Alice") { |name, age| puts "#{name} is #{age} years old." }
```

This results in:

```
Collecting information for Alice:
Alice is 25 years old.
```

Here, the `user_info` method takes a username and yields it alongside a hypothetical age to the block. The block receives these as parameters and uses them in its body. This technique makes methods even more flexible by allowing them to interact with blocks dynamically, adapting their behavior based on both method's input and the logic contained within the block.

In summary, yielding to blocks is a powerful Ruby feature that promotes code reusability, flexibility, and adaptability. By mastering yielding, Ruby developers can create methods that can execute different code blocks according to the context of the call, enhancing the expressiveness and maintainability of Ruby applications.

5.6   Procs and Lambdas: Creating Reusable Code Blocks

Procs and lambdas in Ruby serve the critical function of encapsulating blocks of code into objects that can be passed around and executed. This capability elevates the flexibility and reusability of Ruby code, making it easier to manage and apply in various contexts.

Procs

A Proc object is a block of code that has been bound to a set of local variables. Once bound, the block can be passed to methods and executed. To create a Proc, you can use the Proc.new method or the proc method. Here is an example using Proc.new:

```
say_hello = Proc.new do |name|
  puts "Hello, #{name}"
end
```

To invoke a Proc, the call method is used, as shown below:

```
say_hello.call("Alice")
```

```
Hello, Alice
```

Lambdas

Lambdas in Ruby are similar to Procs but differ in two main aspects: how they handle arguments and their return behavior within a method. To define a lambda, you can use the following syntax:

```
say_goodbye = lambda { |name|
  puts "Goodbye, #{name}"
}
```

Alternatively, Ruby provides a shorthand syntax for lambdas:

```
say_goodbye = ->(name) {
  puts "Goodbye, #{name}"
}
```

Like Procs, lambdas are called using the `call` method:

```
1  say_goodbye.call("Bob")
```

```
Goodbye, Bob
```

Differences Between Procs and Lambdas

Understanding the differences between procs and lambdas is crucial for effectively leveraging them in Ruby applications. The two primary differences are:

- **Argument Handling:** Lambdas check the number of arguments passed to them and will throw an error if the number of arguments does not match the expectation. In contrast, Procs do not enforce the number of arguments.

- **Return Behavior:** When a return statement is executed inside a lambda, it returns control to the calling method. However, if a return statement is executed inside a proc, it will exit from the method enclosing the proc.

When to Use Procs and Lambdas

Choosing between procs and lambdas depends on the specific requirements of your application. Use lambdas when you need strict argument compliance and wish to return control to the calling method after execution. On the other hand, procs are more flexible concerning argument handling and are suitable when you need to exit from the enclosing method upon execution of the block.

In summary, procs and lambdas enhance Ruby's capability for reusing and managing blocks of code. By understanding their characteristics and differences, you can effectively employ these constructs to write clean, maintainable, and flexible Ruby applications.

5.7 Differences Between Procs, Lambdas, and Blocks

Understanding the distinctions among procs, lambdas, and blocks is crucial for Ruby programmers, as each serves a unique role in Ruby's approach to encapsulating and reusing code. Although they share some similarities, such as being able to encapsulate blocks of code for later execution, their behaviors and capabilities differ in notable ways.

First, let's define each term to ensure clarity:

- A block is a chunk of code enclosed between either braces {} or the do...end construct. It is passed to a method as an implicit parameter and can be invoked with the yield statement.

- A proc (short for procedure) is a block of code encapsulated into an object of the Proc class, which can be stored in a variable and passed around.

- A lambda is a variant of Proc. While very similar to procs, lambdas differ in terms of how they handle parameters and return statements.

The key differences among these three constructs can be categorized as follows:

Parameter Handling

When it comes to parameter handling, procs and lambdas exhibit different behaviors. Lambdas check the number of arguments passed and will throw an error if the number of arguments provided does not match the expectation. In contrast, procs are more lenient, allowing for missing arguments without causing runtime errors.

```
1  # Lambda example
2  my_lambda = lambda {|a, b| a + b}
3  my_lambda.call(1, 2) # => 3
4  my_lambda.call(1) # ArgumentError: wrong number of arguments (1 for 2)
```

```
5
6   # Proc example
7   my_proc = Proc.new {|a, b| a + b}
8   my_proc.call(1, 2) # => 3
9   my_proc.call(1) # => nil + b raises an error, but no ArgumentError
```

Return Behavior

Another significant difference lies in how procs and lambdas handle
the return statement. When a return is executed inside a lambda, it
exits the lambda and returns control to the calling method, whereas
a return inside a proc exits the containing method itself.

```
1   def test_lambda
2     my_lambda = lambda { return "return from lambda" }
3     my_lambda.call
4     return "return from method"
5   end
6
7   def test_proc
8     my_proc = Proc.new { return "return from proc" }
9     my_proc.call
10    return "return from method"
11  end
12
13  puts test_lambda # Outputs "return from method"
14  puts test_proc # Outputs "return from proc"
```

Block Binding and Scope

Blocks, unlike procs and lambdas, do not detach the code from its
context, meaning variables and methods outside the block are accessible within it. This characteristic enables blocks to work seamlessly
with iterators and other enumerative methods without requiring explicit parameter passing for context access.

To illustrate:

```
1   external_var = 10
2
3   5.times do |i|
4     puts i + external_var
5   end
```

In this code snippet, the `external_var` is directly accessible within the block passed to `times`, showcasing how blocks maintain their binding to the surrounding context.

Objective Comparison

Finally, it is worth noting the object-oriented nature of `procs` and `lambdas` compared to blocks. Being objects, procs and lambdas can be assigned to variables, stored in data structures, and passed as arguments in a way that blocks cannot without explicit conversion using the & operator.

In summary, while blocks serve as simple, flexible code chunks for inline execution, `procs` offer a more dynamic approach to encapsulating code for reuse, and `lambdas` add a layer of rigor with their strict parameter and return behaviors. Understanding these differences enables programmers to choose the most appropriate tool for each situation, enhancing code clarity, flexibility, and maintainability.

5.8   Passing Blocks, Procs, and Lambdas as Method Arguments

In understanding Ruby, it is critical to grasp how blocks, procs, and lambdas can be passed as arguments to methods. This capability significantly enhances the flexibility and reusability of code.

Blocks as Method Arguments

To start with blocks, recall that blocks are anonymous pieces of code that can be passed to methods to be executed within their context. Generally, to receive a block in a method, Ruby employs the yield keyword. However, when intending to pass a block directly as an argument, it involves prefixing the block parameter with an ampersand (&) operator. This converts the block into a Proc object, allowing it to be stored in a parameter.

```
1  def method_accepting_block(&block)
2    block.call
3  end
4
5  method_accepting_block { puts "Hello, from the block!" }
```

The output of this block of code will be:

```
Hello, from the block!
```

Procs as Method Arguments

Procs, which are Proc objects, encapsulate blocks of code that can be stored in variables and passed around. Unlike blocks, procs can be passed into methods as regular objects without any special syntax.

```
1  def method_accepting_proc(proc)
2    proc.call
3  end
4
5  my_proc = Proc.new { puts "Hello, from the proc!" }
6  method_accepting_proc(my_proc)
```

This proc will produce:

```
Hello, from the proc!
```

Lambdas as Method Arguments

Lambdas in Ruby are akin to procs but with subtle differences, particularly in how they handle return statements and arity (the number of arguments they accept). Just like procs, lambdas can be passed as method arguments straightforwardly.

```
1  def method_accepting_lambda(lambda)
2    lambda.call
3  end
4
5  my_lambda = lambda { puts "Hello, from the lambda!" }
6  method_accepting_lambda(my_lambda)
```

The output for the lambda code snippet is expected to be:

```
Hello, from the lambda!
```

Differences in Handling

Understanding the differences between how blocks, procs, and lambdas are handled when passed to methods illuminates Ruby's flexibility.

- Blocks must be explicitly specified with an ampersand (&) when passed as method arguments. Inside the method, they are converted to a Proc.

- Procs can be passed into methods as plain arguments. There's no need for special syntax unless you're converting a proc to a block using an ampersand (&).

- Lambdas are passed just like procs, but they enforce the arity of parameters more strictly and handle returns differently, making them closer to anonymous functions.

This section has illuminated how Ruby's dynamic nature accommodates different ways of passing executable code segments—blocks, procs, and lambdas—to methods, thus enhancing a developer's toolbox for building expressive and succinct programs.

5.9   Binding and Scoping with Blocks, Procs, and Lambdas

Binding and scoping within the context of blocks, procs, and lambdas in Ruby are crucial concepts that influence how variables and methods are accessed and modified. These features of Ruby allow for flexible and dynamic code but require a clear understanding to avoid unintended behaviors.

Variable Binding in Blocks

Ruby blocks inherit the binding of the context where they are defined. This means that any local variable that is accessible at the point of block definition is also accessible within the block. Consider the following example:

```
1  name = "John"
2  3.times do
3    puts "Hello, #{name}"
4  end
```

```
Hello, John
Hello, John
Hello, John
```

In this case, the local variable name is accessible within the block passed to the times method, illustrating how Ruby blocks preserve the scope of their enclosing environment.

Variable Scoping in Procs and Lambdas

Procs and lambdas, like blocks, also preserve the binding of the context where they are created. This allows them to access local variables from that context. However, there is a difference in how procs and lambdas handle variables that are not defined within their scope.

```
1  def generate_proc
2    value = 42
3    Proc.new { puts value }
4  end
5
6  my_proc = generate_proc
7  my_proc.call
```

```
42
```

In this example, the proc created inside generate_proc is able to access the local variable value, even when called outside of generate_proc's scope. This demonstrates how procs capture their execution context upon definition.

Scoping Rules for Method Definitions

When defining methods within procs, lambdas, or blocks, it is important to note that these methods do not have access to the local variables defined outside their immediate scope. This is because methods in Ruby have their own self-contained scope, separate from the one of procs, lambdas, or blocks. However, instance variables and class variables are accessible since they are bound to the object or class, not to a particular scope of execution.

Overriding Local Variables

Ruby allows blocks, procs, and lambdas to override local variables if they are defined as parameters. This can lead to unexpected behavior if not properly managed. For example:

```
x = 10
[1,2,3].each do |x|
    puts x
end
puts x
```

```
1
2
3
10
```

In this case, the x inside the block shadows the outer x, but only within the scope of the block. After the block, the original x remains unchanged.

Best Practices

Given the flexible yet potentially confusing nature of Ruby's binding and scoping mechanisms, it is advisable to:

- Keep blocks, procs, and lambdas short to easily track variable bindings.

- Avoid modifying external variables within blocks, procs, and lambdas unless explicitly intended.

- Use distinct variable names inside blocks, procs, and lambdas to prevent unintended shadowing.

- Understand the scope of variables, especially when designing libraries or frameworks that extensively use these constructs.

By adhering to these principles, developers can harness the power of Ruby's advanced scoping and binding features without succumbing to their complexities.

This content provides a detailed exploration of how Ruby handles binding and scoping within blocks, procs, and lambdas, offering valuable insights and best practices for developers. Through concise examples and clear explanations, it aims to clarify the behavior of Ruby code in various contexts, ensuring that readers can write clean, understandable, and effective Ruby code.

5.10   The ampersand (&) Operator: Converting Between Blocks and Procs

The ampersand (&) operator in Ruby serves an important purpose in the conversion process between blocks and procs. This section explores the nuances of this operator, illustrating its utility in enabling blocks to be passed as method arguments and how it allows for more dynamic and flexible code structure.

The first aspect to understand is the role of the & operator when used in the context of method definitions and calls. When defining a method that accepts a block, typically, the block is implicitly available and is not named among the method's parameters. However, to convert this block into a proc, allowing it to be stored, passed around, or manipulated, the & operator is prefixed to a parameter name in the method definition.

For example, consider a method that yields to a block:

```
1  def example_method
2    yield if block_given?
3  end
```

If we wish to convert the block passed to this method into a proc, we modify the method definition as follows:

```
1  def example_method(&block)
2    block.call if block
3  end
```

In this revised definition, `block` is now a parameter of the method, holding a proc converted from the passed block, thanks to the & operator. The `block.call` statement then executes the code within the proc.

Conversely, the & operator is employed when passing a proc to a method expecting a block. This practice is necessary because while Ruby methods can implicitly accept blocks, they cannot directly take procs or lambdas without conversion. The & operator, placed before a proc in a method call, converts the proc back to a block.

To demonstrate, consider the following proc definition and method call:

```
1  my_proc = Proc.new { puts "This is a proc being executed!" }
2
3  example_method(&my_proc)
```

The & operator preceding `my_proc` in the method call instructs Ruby to convert `my_proc` from a proc to a block, thereby satisfying the method's expectation for a block argument.

Using the & operator in both method definitions and calls allows for a highly versatile way of handling code blocks. This versatility is especially beneficial in situations where the behavior of a method needs to be customized or when implementing APIs that should be flexible regarding block and proc arguments.

To encapsulate, the & operator's primary functions can be summarized as follows:

- In method definitions, it converts an incoming block into a proc, enabling the block to be referenced, stored, or manipulated as an object within the method.

- In method calls, it converts a proc to a block, allowing procs (or lambdas) to be passed to methods that are designed to take blocks.

This dual functionality underscores the & operator's critical role in Ruby's handling of blocks, procs, and lambdas, facilitating a more dynamic and functional approach to code reusability and manipulation.

5.11   Use Cases for Methods, Blocks, Procs, and Lambdas

Methods in Ruby serve as the foundation for structuring code into reusable and maintainable components. Whether it's performing a calculation, manipulating data, or handling input/output operations, methods encapsulate these routines in a single, callable entity. For example, consider a method that computes the factorial of a number:

```
1  def factorial(n)
2    return 1 if n <= 1
3    n * factorial(n-1)
4  end
```

Blocks, on the other hand, offer flexibility in executing code within the context of a method call. They are particularly useful for iteration and code that requires temporary, dynamic adjustments. A classic use case is iterating over a collection, where a block can be passed to methods like each or map to apply a specific operation to each element:

```
1  [1, 2, 3].map { |number| number * 2 }
```

```
=> [2, 4, 6]
```

124

Procs encapsulate blocks of code that can be stored in variables and passed as arguments, making them ideal for delayed execution or when the same block of code is needed in multiple places. This is particularly useful for callbacks and higher-order functions. A proc can store a block for later execution:

```
1  double = Proc.new { |n| n * 2 }
2  [1, 2, 3].map(&double)
```

```
=> [2, 4, 6]
```

Lambdas, while similar to procs, enforce arity and are more strict in their behavior, making them well-suited for situations where you expect specific inputs and outputs. A lambda that checks if a number is even could be as follows:

```
1  is_even = lambda { |n| n % 2 == 0 }
2  [1, 2, 3, 4].select(&is_even)
```

```
=> [2, 4]
```

The versatility of methods, blocks, procs, and lambdas offers a comprehensive toolkit for Ruby programmers to tackle a wide range of programming tasks, from simple data processing to complex business logic.

- Methods provide a way to encapsulate and organize functionality.

- Blocks allow for inline, anonymous functionality that can be passed to methods.

- Procs offer the flexibility to store and pass around blocks as objects.

- Lambdas provide a concise syntax for defining small functions with strict parameter and return behaviors.

Understanding the appropriate use case for each of these constructs enhances code reusability, modularity, and clarity—a hallmark of proficient Ruby programming.

5.12   Best   Practices   for   Structure   and Readability

In this section, we will discuss recommended strategies to enhance the structure and readability of Ruby codes when utilizing methods, blocks, procs, and lambdas. The objective is to ensure that your code is not only functional but also easy to read, maintain, and refactor. By adhering to these practices, programmers can produce code that is more accessible to others and themselves, facilitating collaboration and reducing the likelihood of errors.

1. Consistent Naming Conventions

Following consistent naming conventions is crucial in making your code understandable. Ruby employs snake_case for method and variable names. This should also apply when you define methods, procs, and lambdas.

```
1  # Good practice
2  def calculate_total_price
3    # Method logic here
4  end
5
6  bad_proc_name = Proc.new { |x| puts x }
7  # Better practice
8  good_proc_name = Proc.new { |x| puts x }
```

2. Limiting Method Length

Methods should be concise and perform a single responsibility. If a method exceeds 10 lines of code, consider breaking it down into smaller, more-focused helper methods. This approach not only makes the code more readable but also facilitates testing and debugging.

```
1  # Before refactoring
2  def process_data_and_generate_report
3    # Approximately 20 lines of code combining data processing and report
          generation
4  end
```

```
 5
 6  # After refactoring
 7  def process_data
 8    # Code focused solely on data processing
 9  end
10
11  def generate_report
12    # Code focused solely on report generation
13  end
```

3. Documenting with Comments

While Ruby's syntax is designed to be readable, complex logic can sometimes be difficult to understand at a glance. Use comments judiciously to explain the "why" behind non-obvious design decisions or complex algorithms. Remember, code tells you how, comments should tell you why.

```
1  def fibonacci(n)
2    # Base case: return n if n is 0 or 1
3    return n if n <= 1
4    # Recursive call for Fibonacci sequence
5    fibonacci(n-1) + fibonacci(n-2)
6  end
```

4. Effective Use of Blocks, Procs, and Lambdas

Blocks, procs, and lambdas offer great flexibility but can lead to readability issues if not used carefully. Use blocks for simple, single-use operations; procs for reusable code blocks that might be passed around a few times; and lambdas when you need the functionality of procs but with strict argument checking.

- Use blocks with methods like .each for iterating over collections.

- Prefer procs when you need to store a block to pass as a method argument multiple times.

- Use lambdas for more complex functionalities that benefit from argument count enforcement.

```
1  # Using a block
2  [1, 2, 3].each { |number| puts number }
3
4  # Defining a proc
5  reusable_block = Proc.new { |number| puts number }
6  [1, 2, 3].each(&reusable_block)
7
8  # Defining a lambda
9  strict_block = lambda { |number| puts number if number.is_a?(Integer) }
10 [1, 2, 3].each(&strict_block)
```

5. Handling Variable-Length Arguments Wisely

Ruby's ability to handle variable-length arguments using splat (*)
and double splat (**) operators is powerful but should be used
judiciously. Overuse can make method signatures unclear and the
code difficult to understand. Employ these operators primarily
when the number of arguments genuinely varies, enhancing the
method's flexibility without sacrificing readability.

```
1  def dynamic_greeting(*names)
2    names.each { |name| puts "Hello, #{name}!" }
3  end
4
5  dynamic_greeting('Alice', 'Bob', 'Carol')
```

6. Adhering to the Law of Demeter

The Law of Demeter, a design guideline for developing software,
suggests that a method should call other methods belonging to its
immediate object rather than reaching through objects to invoke
methods on a distant object. Following this guideline can enhance
encapsulation and reduce coupling within your code.

```
1  # Violating the Law of Demeter
2  def display_user_location
3    puts @user.profile.address.zipcode
4  end
5
6  # Adhering to the Law of Demeter
7  def display_user_location
8    puts @user.zipcode
9  end
```

```
10
11   # Assuming @user has a method #zipcode that abstracts the details
```

By embedding these best practices into your workflow, you can significantly improve the structure and readability of your Ruby projects, leading to code that is more maintainable, understandable, and clean. Remember, the goal is to write code that not only computers can execute but also humans can easily read and understand.

Chapter 6

Object-Oriented Programming in Ruby

This chapter explores Ruby's implementation of object-oriented programming (OOP), a paradigm centered around objects and classes that enables developers to structure their programs more effectively. It introduces the concepts of classes and objects, the blueprint and instances respectively, and goes on to discuss class methods, instance methods, inheritance, polymorphism, and modules. Through these concepts, Ruby allows for encapsulating data and behavior within objects, fostering a design that is both modular and reusable. Understanding OOP principles within the context of Ruby is crucial for leveraging the language's full potential in building scalable and maintainable applications.

6.1 Introduction to Object-Oriented Programming (OOP)

Object-Oriented Programming, commonly referred to as OOP, stands as a foundational pillar in the realm of software development. This programming paradigm is distinguished by its use of classes and objects, empowering developers to conceive their software structures not merely as sequences of procedures or instructions but as living, interactive entities. In Ruby, OOP is not just supported; it's ingrained into the very core of the language, making it an essential concept for Ruby developers to grasp.

At the heart of OOP lies the concept of an *object*. An object is a self-contained component that contains properties and behaviors, which are defined by the object's class. A class, then, can be thought of as a blueprint or template from which objects are created. This facilitates a higher level of abstraction in program design, enabling programmers to work with real-world concepts within the code. To illustrate this, consider the following Ruby code snippet defining a simple class and generating an object from it:

```
1   class Dog
2     def initialize(name, breed)
3       @name = name
4       @breed = breed
5     end
6
7     def bark
8       puts "Woof!"
9     end
10  end
11
12  my_dog = Dog.new("Rex", "Shepherd")
```

In the above example, Dog is a class that includes an initialization method initialize and a behavior method bark. The @name and @breed variables are instance variables, exclusive to each instance of the Dog class. my_dog is an instance of the Dog class, created with the .new method, which invocates the initialize method of the class.

OOP introduces several key concepts critical for a robust understanding:

- *Encapsulation*: This concept is about bundling the data (attributes) and the methods (functions or operations) that operate on the data into a single unit, or class, and controlling access to the inner workings of the class from the outside. In Ruby, this is commonly implemented through the use of public, protected, and private access modifiers.

- *Inheritance*: Inheritance allows new classes to adopt the properties and methods of existing classes. This relationship not only facilitates code reuse but also creates a hierarchical classification of classes. In Ruby, inheritance is denoted by the < symbol.

- *Polymorphism*: Polymorphism grants the ability to treat different objects—provided they share certain properties or methods—as interchangeable. Ruby implements polymorphism primarily through duck typing, whereby an object's suitability is determined by the presence of specific methods rather than by its class.

- *Modules*: Unlike some other languages, Ruby supports single inheritance only. However, Ruby's modules allow for the sharing of methods across multiple classes, acting as a hybrid between classes and namespaces. Modules can also be mixed into classes using the `include` method.

Each of these concepts contributes to the overall philosophy of OOP, focusing on creating more modular, reusable, and manageable code. By constructing software from a collection of interacting objects, developers can mirror real-world systems more closely, promoting both clarity and flexibility in the program's architecture.

Understanding these foundational concepts is crucial for any developer working with Ruby or any OOP language, as they form the basis for Ruby's approach to software development. With this foundation, the subsequent sections will delve deeper into each of these concepts, exploring how they are implemented in Ruby and how developers can leverage them to build sophisticated, robust applications.

6.2 Classes and Objects in Ruby

In Ruby, classes serve as the blueprint from which objects, the fundamental building blocks, are created. A class encapsulates both data-related attributes and methods for manipulating that data, effectively modeling real-world entities within a program's structure.

To define a class in Ruby, we use the class keyword followed by the class name, adhering to the convention of beginning each word with a capital letter (CamelCase). The end of a class definition is marked with the end keyword. Let's illustrate this with a simple example:

```
1  class Vehicle
2    # class body encompassing attributes and methods
3  end
```

Within this class structure, we can introduce instance variables to hold data. Instance variables in Ruby are prefixed with an '@' symbol. To initialize an object of a class with specific data, Ruby provides a special method named initialize. This method is automatically invoked when an object is created using the new method.

```
1  class Vehicle
2    def initialize(model, year)
3      @model = model
4      @year = year
5    end
6  end
```

To create an object, or an instance of the class, we make use of the new method along with any arguments required by the initialize method, as shown below:

```
1  my_car = Vehicle.new('Toyota Camry', 2020)
```

In the above example, my_car is an instance of the Vehicle class, encapsulating the model and year data within its structure.

Ruby also allows for defining methods within a class to perform operations on the instance variables. These are known as instance methods. Consider extending the Vehicle class to include a method to display information about the vehicle:

```
1  class Vehicle
2    def initialize(model, year)
3      @model = model
4      @year = year
```

```
 5   end
 6
 7   def display_info
 8     puts "Model: #{@model}, Year: #{@year}"
 9   end
10  end
11
12  my_car.display_info
```

When `display_info` is called on the `my_car` object, the output will be:

```
Model: Toyota Camry, Year: 2020
```

Classes in Ruby also provide mechanisms for defining class variables and class methods. Class variables are shared across all instances of a class and are prefixed with . Class methods, on the other hand, are methods that are called on the class itself, not on individual objects. They are defined by prefixing the method name with `self`.

```
 1  class Vehicle
 2    @@total_vehicles = 0
 3
 4    def initialize(model, year)
 5      @model = model
 6      @year = year
 7      @@total_vehicles += 1
 8    end
 9
10    def self.total_vehicles
11      @@total_vehicles
12    end
13  end
14
15  Vehicle.new('Toyota Camry', 2020)
16  Vehicle.new('Honda Civic', 2019)
17  puts Vehicle.total_vehicles
```

The output of calling `Vehicle.total_vehicles` will be:

```
2
```

This concludes an initial exploration into classes and objects in Ruby, showcasing the capacity to model real-world entities and behaviors within a program's structure. This foundation is essential for understanding more advanced OOP concepts such as inheritance, polymorphism, and modules which are discussed in subsequent sections.

6.3 Defining Class Methods and Variables

In this section, we will discuss how to define class methods and variables in Ruby, which is a powerful feature of object-oriented programming. Class methods and variables are associated with the class itself, rather than any instance of the class.

Class Variables: These are variables that are shared among all instances of a class. They begin with two '@' symbols (e.g., '@@name'). Class variables are useful for storing information relevant to all objects of a class.

However, one should exercise caution while using class variables due to their shared nature, which can lead to unexpected results if not managed properly. For example, altering a class variable in one instance will affect all other instances of the class.

The following is an example of defining and accessing a class variable in Ruby:

```ruby
class Vehicle
  @@number_of_vehicles = 0

  def initialize
    @@number_of_vehicles += 1
  end

  def self.total_vehicles
    @@number_of_vehicles
  end
end

car = Vehicle.new
truck = Vehicle.new
puts Vehicle.total_vehicles
```

The `total_vehicles` class method returns the total number of instances created from the `Vehicle` class. The output of the above code would be:

```
2
```

Class Methods: Just like instance methods belong to instances of a class, class methods belong to the class itself. They are called on the class, not on instances of the class. You define a class method by prefixing the method name with 'self'.

The purpose of class methods can range from returning class-specific information to providing factory methods that return objects of the class. Here's how you define and call a class method:

```
 1   class User
 2     @@users_count = 0
 3
 4     def initialize
 5       @@users_count += 1
 6     end
 7
 8     def self.count
 9       @@users_count
10     end
11   end
12
13   User.new
14   User.new
15   puts User.count
```

This code snippet defines a User class with a class variable '@@users_count' and a class method 'self.count'. Every time a new User instance is created, '@@users_count' is incremented. The User.count class method returns the total number of User instances created. The output here would be:

2

Understanding and properly utilizing class methods and variables are fundamental to effective object-oriented programming in Ruby. They enable behaviors and data that are relevant to the entire class rather than individual instances, offering a different level of abstraction and utility.

6.4 Instance Methods and Variables

Instance methods and variables are fundamental to object-oriented programming in Ruby, enabling objects to carry out specific functionalities and to hold individual state information respectively. This sec-

137

tion will delineate how to define and use instance methods and variables within classes, exemplifying their importance in crafting object-specific behaviors and attributes.

Defining Instance Variables

Instance variables in Ruby are denoted by prefixing the variable name with an '@' symbol. These variables are unique to each instance of a class, meaning that each object created from the same class can have different values for the same instance variable. Below is an illustration of how to define instance variables within a class.

```
1   class Car
2     def initialize(model, color)
3       @model = model
4       @color = color
5     end
6   end
```

In the example above, @model and @color are instance variables of the Car class. The initialize method is a special method in Ruby that gets called whenever a new instance of the class is created. It is used here to set the initial values of the instance variables.

Accessing Instance Variables

Access to instance variables is limited within the object's scope; they cannot be accessed directly from outside the object. To interact with instance variables, accessor methods must be defined or generated. Ruby provides a convenient way to automatically create these methods using the attr_accessor, attr_reader, and attr_writer symbols as shown below.

```
1   class Car
2     attr_accessor :model, :color
3
4     def initialize(model, color)
5       @model = model
6       @color = color
7     end
8   end
```

The `attr_accessor` symbol generates both reader and writer methods for the specified instance variables, enabling their values to be retrieved and modified from outside the object. If only read or write functionalities are needed, `attr_reader` and `attr_writer` can be used respectively.

Defining Instance Methods

Instance methods define behaviors for class instances. Unlike instance variables, instance methods are accessible from outside the object. The syntax for defining an instance method is similar to defining any method in Ruby, as illustrated below.

```
1   class Car
2     attr_accessor :model, :color
3
4     def initialize(model, color)
5       @model = model
6       @color = color
7     end
8
9     def describe
10      "This is a \#{@model} car and its color is \#{@color}."
11    end
12  end
13
14  my_car = Car.new('Tesla', 'red')
15  puts my_car.describe
```

In the above example, the `describe` method is an instance method of the Car class. It utilizes the instance variables `@model` and `@color` to return a string that describes the car. The instance method can be called on any object of the Car class, as demonstrated with the `my_car` object.

```
This is a Tesla car and its color is red.
```

Through instance methods and variables, Ruby facilitates the encapsulation and manipulation of individual object states and behaviors, providing a powerful tool for creating sophisticated and modular object-oriented programs.

6.5   Access Control: Public,   Protected,   and Private Methods

Access control mechanisms in Ruby serve to delineate the level of visibility for methods within classes. They define how and where methods can be called, playing a critical role in object-oriented programming by ensuring that the internal state of an object is safeguarded from unintended modifications and interactions. Ruby implements three primary levels of access control: public, protected, and private methods.

Public Methods

Public methods in Ruby are the default class methods. They are accessible from any part of the program and can be called by any object. This level of visibility is often applied to interfaces of a class - methods intended to be accessible to the rest of the application.

```
1  class SampleClass
2    def public_method
3      puts "I'm a public method!"
4    end
5  end
6
7  object = SampleClass.new
8  object.public_method # Output: I'm a public method!
```

Protected Methods

Protected methods strike a balance between the openness of public methods and the restrictiveness of private methods. A protected method in Ruby is only accessible within its defining class and its subclasses. Unlike private methods, however, protected methods can be called by any instance of the defining class or its subclasses, not just by the instance that is the receiver of the current method.

```
1  class ParentClass
2    protected
3
```

```
4    def protected_method
5      "I'm a protected method!"
6    end
7  end
8
9  class ChildClass < ParentClass
10    def call_protected_method(other)
11      puts other.protected_method
12    end
13  end
14
15  parent = ParentClass.new
16  child = ChildClass.new
17  child.call_protected_method(parent)
18  # Output: I'm a protected method!
```

Private Methods

Private methods in Ruby are designed to be the most restrictive access level. They can only be called by other methods within the same class and cannot be accessed directly by an object instance. This access level is instrumental in encapsulating behavior that should not be exposed outside of the class.

```
1  class ExampleClass
2    def public_method
3      puts "Public method is calling private method."
4      private_method
5    end
6
7    private
8
9    def private_method
10      puts "I'm a private method!"
11    end
12  end
13
14  object = ExampleClass.new
15  object.public_method
16  # Output: Public method is calling private method.
17  # I'm a private method!
18  object.private_method # NoMethodError
```

Changing Method Access Levels

Ruby also provides flexibility in modifying the access control of methods using the public, protected, and private keywords. Methods defined after these keywords will have the specified access

141

level unless another access control keyword is encountered.

```
1   class MyClass
2     def method1; "This is public"; end
3     def method2; "This is initially public"; end
4
5     private :method2
6
7     def method3; "This is also public"; end
8   end
9
10  object = MyClass.new
11  puts object.method1 # Output: This is public
12  puts object.method2 # NoMethodError
13  puts object.method3 # Output: This is also public
```

To preserve the integrity and design of Ruby programs, leveraging the proper level of access control is paramount. Each level has its application scenarios and understanding when to use each can greatly enhance the quality and security of your code. Through the judicious use of public, protected, and private methods, developers can enforce encapsulation and promote a robust, maintainable codebase.

6.6   Inheritance in Ruby: Extending Classes

Inheritance is a fundamental concept in object-oriented programming that Ruby implements proficiently, allowing developers to create a hierarchy of classes. In essence, a subclass inherits methods and attributes from a parent class, enhancing code reusability and maintainability. This section elucidates Ruby's approach to inheritance, detailing syntax, usage, and nuances that ensure a profound understanding.

Let's start with the basic syntax for defining a class that inherits from another. Consider the scenario where we have a general Vehicle class, and we wish to define a more specific Car class that inherits from Vehicle.

```
1   class Vehicle
2     def initialize(name, speed)
3       @name = name
4       @speed = speed
```

```
 5    end
 6
 7    def move
 8      puts "#{@name} is moving at #{@speed} mph."
 9    end
10  end
11
12  class Car < Vehicle
13    def initialize(name, speed, mpg)
14      super(name, speed)
15      @mpg = mpg
16    end
17
18    def display_efficiency
19      puts "The #{@name} moves at #{@speed} mph and gets #{@mpg} miles per gallon."
20    end
21  end
```

In the example above, the Car class uses the < symbol to inherit from the Vehicle class. By calling super inside Car's initialize method, Ruby knows to execute the initialize method of the Vehicle class, allowing Car instances to also have name and speed attributes in addition to mpg.

However, inheritance is not merely about reusing code from the superclass. It also introduces the concept of method overriding, where a subclass can redefine certain methods inherited from the parent class.

```
 1  class ElectricCar < Car
 2    def initialize(name, speed, battery_range)
 3      super(name, speed, 0) # Electric cars don't consume traditional mpg
 4      @battery_range = battery_range
 5    end
 6
 7    def display_efficiency
 8      puts "The #{@name} moves at #{@speed} mph and has a range of #{@battery_range
         } miles on a full charge."
 9    end
10  end
```

In the ElectricCar class, display_efficiency is overridden to be more relevant for electric vehicles, emphasizing the battery range instead of miles per gallon. This demonstrates how Ruby's inheritance mechanism can be customized to fit the specific needs of subclasses while still leveraging the functionality of their ancestors.

Next, consider the importance of understanding inheritance hierarchy. Ruby provides a simple method to inspect this: .ancestors.

```
1   puts ElectricCar.ancestors
```

```
[ElectricCar, Car, Vehicle, Object, Kernel, BasicObject]
```

The output shows the chain of inheritance from ElectricCar all the way up to BasicObject, Ruby's most basic class. This hierarchy is vital when dealing with method look-up paths, as Ruby searches up this chain to find the first instance of a method name when a method is called.

To summarize, Ruby's inheritance allows for the elegant extension of classes, promoting DRY (Don't Repeat Yourself) principles and facilitating a polymorphic design. Through inheritance, subclasses can not only reuse and extend the capabilities of parent classes but also tailor inherited behavior to fit their specific context, making Ruby's take on object-oriented programming both powerful and flexible.

6.7   Polymorphism and Duck Typing

Polymorphism, derived from the Greek words "poly" meaning many and "morph" meaning forms, is a fundamental concept in object-oriented programming that allows objects of different classes to be treated as objects of a common super class. The essence of polymorphism in Ruby lies in its ability to send the same message (or invoke a method) on objects of different types and have each object respond in a way appropriate to its type.

In Ruby, polymorphism is commonly achieved through two mechanisms: inheritance and duck typing. While inheritance is a well-understood concept wherein a subclass inherits behavior from a superclass and can override or extend this behavior, duck typing is a unique feature of dynamically typed languages like Ruby.

Duck Typing in Ruby

The principle of duck typing is succinctly captured in the adage, "If it walks like a duck and quacks like a duck, then it must be a duck". Translated to programming, this means that an object's suitability for a task is determined by the presence of certain methods and properties rather than by the object's class. Ruby, being a dynamically typed language, embraces duck typing, enabling a more flexible and less tightly coupled code.

Consider the following example illustrating duck typing:

```
1   def play_sound(animal)
2     animal.quack
3   end
4
5   class Duck
6     def quack
7       puts "Quack!"
8     end
9   end
10
11  class Dog
12    def quack
13      puts "Woof! (but in a quacky way)"
14    end
15  end
16
17  duck = Duck.new
18  dog = Dog.new
19
20  play_sound(duck)
21  play_sound(dog)
```

In the example above, the `play_sound` method expects an object that responds to the quack method. It does not matter whether the object is an instance of Duck or Dog; as long as the object can respond to quack, it can be passed to `play_sound`. The corresponding output for the code above is:

```
Quack!
Woof! (but in a quacky way)
```

This example showcases the flexibility of duck typing: by focusing on what an object does rather than what it is, Ruby allows for more generic and reusable code. It's important to note, however, that

145

while duck typing can increase flexibility, it also requires the developer to ensure that objects fulfill the expected contracts (i.e., respond to the correct methods) since these contracts are not enforced by the language syntax.

Duck typing extends to more than just method names; it encompasses the overall behavior of an object. If an object fulfills all the requirements to "act as" another object, then it can be used in any context where the latter is expected. This principle allows for the creation of highly modular and decoupled systems where individual components can be easily replaced as long as they conform to the expected behavior.

In summary, polymorphism and duck typing in Ruby offer powerful mechanisms for writing flexible, modular code. By allowing one to focus on the capabilities of objects rather than their class hierarchy, Ruby fosters a development approach that is more focused on behavior and less on the rigid categorization of objects.

6.8   Modules as Namespaces and Mixins

In Ruby, modules serve two primary purposes: as namespaces and as mixins. Before diving into the specifics of each use case, it is important to understand what a module is. A module is a collection of methods and constants. They cannot be instantiated like classes and do not support inheritance. However, they play a pivotal role in organizing code and avoiding naming collisions, as well as sharing functionality across classes.

Modules as Namespaces

Using modules as namespaces is a strategy to encapsulate related classes, methods, and constants within a unique scope. This encapsulation helps to prevent name clashes between identifiers that might otherwise have the same name but serve different purposes. Consider the following example:

```
1    module Transportation
2      class Vehicle
3        # Vehicle definition here
4      end
5
6      class Car < Vehicle
7        # Car definition here
8      end
9    end
```

In this instance, both Vehicle and Car are encapsulated within the Transportation module. This means that to reference the Car class, one would need to prefix it with the module name, creating a fully qualified name: Transportation::Car. This approach effectively namespaces the classes and lets you have another Car class elsewhere in your program without conflict.

Modules as Mixins

A mixin is a way to add functionality to a class from a module, rather than inheriting from another class. This is particularly valuable in Ruby, where classes can only inherit from a single superclass. Mixins allow for the sharing of methods across classes without requiring a hierarchical relationship. To include module's methods as instance methods in a class, use the include keyword. To include them as class methods, use the extend keyword.

Consider the following example, which demonstrates the use of a mixin to add a common behavior to different classes:

```
1    module Drivable
2      def drive
3        puts "This vehicle is driving."
4      end
5    end
6
7    class Car
8      include Drivable
9    end
10
11   class Motorcycle
12     include Drivable
13   end
```

Here, both Car and Motorcycle classes include the Drivable module.

147

This means instances of both classes have access to the `drive` method. This is an excellent example of code reuse through mixins, negating the need for duplicated code across classes that share behavior.

It is crucial to understand that when a module is used as a mixin, the methods included or extended become part of the class that includes or extends the module, thus adhering to the object's inheritance chain.

Best Practices for Using Modules

When incorporating modules into your Ruby applications, keep the following practices in mind:

- Use namespaces to logically group related classes and prevent naming conflicts.

- Employ mixins to share reusable code across classes, enhancing the DRY (Don't Repeat Yourself) principle.

- Maintain clarity and organization by using modules judiciously, avoiding overly complex inheritance hierarchies.

In summary, modules in Ruby offer powerful mechanisms for both namespacing and sharing functionality. By understanding and applying these concepts, developers can create more organized, modular, and maintainable Ruby applications.

6.9   The self Keyword in Context

Understanding the `self` keyword in Ruby is instrumental in accurately navigating both class and instance contexts within object-oriented programming. The `self` keyword serves a dual purpose: it references the current instance of a class or the class itself, depending on the context in which it is used.

Instance Context

When self is used within an instance method, it refers to the instance (object) that invoked the method. This is particularly useful for specifying that method calls and attribute access should occur on the current object.

Consider the following example:

```
 1  class Person
 2    attr_accessor :name
 3
 4    def initialize(name)
 5      @name = name
 6    end
 7
 8    def print_name
 9      puts "Name: #{self.name}"
10    end
11  end
12
13  person = Person.new("Alice")
14  person.print_name
```

In the print_name method, self.name is equivalent to @name, but it uses the name getter method provided by attr_accessor instead of directly accessing the instance variable. This encapsulates the access to @name, allowing any special processing defined in the name method to be automatically applied.

Class Context

In the context of a class method or inside the class definition but outside any instance methods, self refers to the class itself. This allows for the definition of class methods and class variables, as well as for class-specific functionality to be encapsulated within the class definition.

Here is an example illustrating self in a class context:

```
 1  class Calculator
 2    @calculation_count = 0
 3
 4    def self.increment_count
 5      @calculation_count += 1
 6    end
```

149

```
 7
 8    def self.calculation_count
 9      @calculation_count
10    end
11
12    def add(a, b)
13      self.class.increment_count
14      a + b
15    end
16  end
17
18  calc = Calculator.new
19  puts calc.add(5, 10)
20  puts Calculator.calculation_count
```

In   this   example,   `self.increment_count`   and
`self.calculation_count` within the class methods refer to the
Calculator class itself, enabling the management of class-level data
like the calculation count. The `self.class` call within an instance
method points to the class (Calculator) that the instance belongs to,
thus allowing an instance to interact with class-level methods and
properties.

The Role of `self` in Context Switching

`self` is pivotal for distinguishing between instance and class
contexts, especially when the same names are used in both scopes.
It clarifies where methods should be invoked and where attributes
are being accessed, leading to code that is more readable and less
prone to errors typical of context confusion.

In summary, mastering the use of `self` is crucial for effectively leveraging Ruby's object-oriented capabilities, enhancing both the robustness and clarity of code.

6.10   Working with Singleton Methods and Classes

In Ruby, singleton methods and classes provide a distinctive way of
adding functionality to individual objects, and crafting classes that

are only meant to have one instance. This concept is paramount for certain design patterns, and understanding its implementation in Ruby is crucial for advanced software development.

Defining Singleton Methods

A singleton method is an instance method that is defined for a single object rather than a class of objects. The syntax for defining a singleton method in Ruby is straightforward:

```
1   object = Object.new
2
3   def object.singleton_method
4     puts "This is a singleton method"
5   end
6
7   object.singleton_method
```

When the above code is executed, the output will be:

```
This is a singleton method
```

By defining a method this way, it becomes exclusively available to the object instance. Other instances of the same class will not have access to this method.

Singleton Classes

To understand singleton methods, it's crucial to comprehend the underlying mechanism of singleton classes (also known as eigenclasses). Every object in Ruby has an invisible, unique singleton class that sits in its inheritance chain. It is in this singleton class that Ruby defines the singleton methods. This design allows each object to have unique methods not shared by other objects of the same class.

To add multiple methods to an object, or to manipulate its singleton class directly, Ruby provides the class << self syntax:

```
1   object = Object.new
2
```

```
3   class << object
4     def first_singleton_method
5       puts "First singleton method"
6     end
7
8     def second_singleton_method
9       puts "Second singleton method"
10    end
11  end
12
13  object.first_singleton_method
14  object.second_singleton_method
```

The execution of this code snippet results in:

```
First singleton method
Second singleton method
```

This approach consolidates the definition of singleton methods and is especially useful when defining many singleton methods on the same object.

Singleton Class Usage Scenarios

Singleton classes and methods are particularly useful in several scenarios, including, but not limited to:

- Implementing the Singleton pattern where a class is designed to have only one instance throughout the application.

- Adding methods to an object on-the-fly for metaprogramming purposes.

- Overriding a method for a specific object without affecting other instances of the same class.

To demonstrate a case of the Singleton pattern in Ruby, consider the following implementation:

```
1   require 'singleton'
2
3   class AppConfig
4     include Singleton
```

```
 5
 6    attr_accessor :configuration
 7
 8  end
 9
10  app_config = AppConfig.instance
11  app_config.configuration = { theme: 'dark', version: '1.0' }
12
13  another_config = AppConfig.instance
14  puts another_config.configuration
```

This example uses Ruby's Singleton module from the standard library. The AppConfig class includes Singleton, which ensures that only one instance of AppConfig can be created. Calling AppConfig.instance always returns the same object, ensuring the Singleton pattern is properly enforced.

The output of the code will confirm that both app_config and another_config refer to the same instance:

```
{:theme=>"dark", :version=>"1.0"}
```

Through singleton methods and classes, Ruby provides a powerful feature set for object-specific behavior and the Singleton design pattern, fitting seamlessly into Ruby's object-oriented model and enabling elegant solutions to common software design challenges.

6.11   Composition Over Inheritance

In the field of object-oriented programming, developers often face the dilemma of choosing between composition and inheritance to structure their applications. Within the Ruby programming context, composition is favored over inheritance for various reasons, primarily due to its flexibility and the ease of maintaining code. This section elucidates the concept of composition in Ruby, explains why it is often preferred over inheritance, and demonstrates its practical application through examples.

Composition involves building classes by incorporating other classes or modules, rather than inheriting from them. This approach allows developers to create objects that are compositions of various capabilities provided by different classes or modules. The key principle here is "has-a" relationship as opposed to the "is-a" relationship that inheritance suggests. For clarity, consider an example involving a Library and Books:

```ruby
class Book
  attr_accessor :title, :author

  def initialize(title, author)
    @title = title
    @author = author
  end
end

class Library
  attr_accessor :books

  def initialize
    @books = []
  end

  def add_book(book)
    books << book
  end

  def list_books
    books.each { |book| puts "Title: #{book.title}, Author: #{book.author}" }
  end
end
```

In the example above, a Library consists of Books. The Library class uses composition by containing and managing instances of the Book class, rather than inheriting from it. This design offers several advantages:

- Flexibility: Changes to the Book class do not affect the Library class, and vice versa, promoting loose coupling.

- Reusability: The Book class can be reused in different contexts without the need for subclassing, which can lead to a rigid hierarchy.

- Simplicity: Avoids the complexity of deep inheritance hierarchies, making the code easier to understand and maintain.

Contrastingly, inheritance establishes an "is-a" relationship between a base class and derived classes. However, it can sometimes introduce unnecessary rigidity and complexity into an application's design. Deep inheritance hierarchies can make the code difficult to navigate and modify, as changes to the base class may unintentionally affect all subclasses. Therefore, Rubyists often advocate for using composition over inheritance when possible to maintain a more flexible and maintainable codebase.

To further emphasize this point, consider the refactoring of an existing class hierarchy into a composition-based design. Suppose we initially have a system with a deep class hierarchy that represents different types of vehicles. By re-evaluating the common features and behaviors, we can identify components that can be extracted and managed separately through composition. For instance, instead of having Car and Truck classes inherit from a Vehicle class, we can create separate classes for shared components like Engine or Wheels and integrate them into Car and Truck as needed.

While inheritance remains a fundamental concept in object-oriented programming, the principle of composition over inheritance offers a powerful tool for organizing and designing Ruby applications. By favoring composition, developers can achieve greater flexibility, reusability, and modularity in their code, leading to more robust and maintainable software.

6.12 Common OOP Design Patterns Implemented in Ruby

Design patterns are established solutions to common problems encountered in software design. In Ruby, leveraging object-oriented programming (OOP) principles, these patterns provide a template for solving similar design issues. This section delves into some of the most prevalent OOP design patterns and their implementation in Ruby including the Singleton Pattern, Factory Method, Strategy Pattern, Observer Pattern, and Decorator Pattern.

Singleton Pattern

The Singleton Pattern ensures a class has only one instance and provides a global point of access to it. This pattern is useful for scenarios where exactly one object is needed to coordinate actions across the system - for example, a configuration manager for an application.

Implementing the Singleton Pattern in Ruby is straightforward, thanks to the `singleton` module. To create a singleton class, include the `singleton` module in your class definition.

```
1  require 'singleton'
2
3  class ConfigurationManager
4    include Singleton
5  end
```

With this setup, trying to create a new instance of `ConfigurationManager` using `ConfigurationManager.new` will result in an error. Instead, `ConfigurationManager.instance` should be used to get the singleton instance.

Factory Method

The Factory Method Pattern provides an interface for creating objects in a superclass but allows subclasses to alter the type of objects that will be created. This pattern is particularly useful when there is a need to manage or organize a group of related objects.

To implement the Factory Method in Ruby, define an interface in the parent class with a method that creates objects, then override the method in the subclass to return a different type of object.

```
1  class Creator
2    def factory_method
3      raise NotImplementedError, "Factory method should be implemented"
4    end
5
6    def call_factory_method
7      product = factory_method
8      product.action
9    end
10  end
11
12  class ConcreteCreatorA < Creator
```

```
13    def factory_method
14      ConcreteProductA.new
15    end
16  end
17
18  class ConcreteProductA
19    def action
20      puts "Product A action"
21    end
22  end
```

Strategy Pattern

The Strategy Pattern defines a family of algorithms, encapsulates each one, and makes them interchangeable. This allows the algorithm to vary independently from clients that use it.

In Ruby, the Strategy Pattern can be implemented by defining a context class and specific strategy classes. The context class holds a reference to one of the strategies and delegates it executing the algorithm.

```
1  class Context
2    attr_accessor :strategy
3
4    def initialize(strategy)
5      @strategy = strategy
6    end
7
8    def execute_strategy
9      @strategy.do_algorithm
10   end
11 end
12
13 class ConcreteStrategyA
14   def do_algorithm
15     puts "Executing strategy A"
16   end
17 end
```

Observer Pattern

The Observer Pattern defines a one-to-many dependency between objects so that when one object changes state, all its dependents are notified and updated automatically.

Ruby facilitates the Observer Pattern through the observer module. To use it, include Observable in the subject class and override the initialize method to call super.

```
require 'observer'

class Product
  include Observable

  def update_price(price)
    @price = price
    changed
    notify_observers(self)
  end
end
```

Decorator Pattern

The Decorator Pattern allows behavior to be added to an individual object, either statically or dynamically, without affecting the behavior of other objects from the same class.

The following Ruby code illustrates a simple implementation of the Decorator Pattern.

```
class BaseComponent
  def operation
    "Base Component"
  end
end

class Decorator < BaseComponent
  def initialize(component)
    @component = component
  end

  def operation
    @component.operation
  end
end
```

These design patterns exemplify the robustness of Ruby's object-oriented capabilities. By understanding and applying these patterns, Ruby developers can build flexible, scalable, and maintainable applications efficiently.

Chapter 7

Error Handling and Debugging

This chapter addresses the critical aspects of error handling and debugging in Ruby, essential skills for developing robust and error-free applications. It begins with an overview of Ruby's exception mechanism, exploring how to handle errors gracefully using begin, rescue, and ensure blocks. The chapter then shifts focus to raising custom exceptions and creating custom exception classes, providing strategies for more specific error handling. Debugging techniques, including the use of Ruby's built-in debugger tools and best practices for identifying and fixing bugs, are discussed to equip developers with the ability to diagnose and resolve issues effectively, enhancing the stability and reliability of their Ruby applications.

7.1   Understanding Ruby Exceptions

Understanding Ruby exceptions is foundational for writing resilient applications that can gracefully manage errors without crashing. Exceptions in Ruby serve as a mechanism to signal the occurrence

159

of an unexpected event during the execution of a program, allowing the developer to take appropriate action rather than allowing the program to terminate unexpectedly.

In Ruby, exceptions are instances of the class Exception or descendants of this class. This hierarchy enables the creation of specific exception types to handle different error conditions more precisely. The process involves three main components:

- **Raising an exception:** This occurs when a specific error condition is encountered during the execution of a program. Ruby either raises a built-in exception automatically or allows the developer to raise a custom exception using the raise keyword.

- **Handling an exception:** Once an exception is raised, Ruby searches for a matching begin-rescue block to handle the exception. If a matching exception type is found within a rescue clause, the code within that clause is executed, allowing for recovery from the error condition.

- **Ensuring execution:** The ensure block can be used alongside begin-rescue to ensure that certain cleanup code is executed, regardless of whether an exception was raised and handled or not.

Let's illustrate the process with a simple example. Consider a scenario where we want to read a file and print its content to the console:

```
1   def read_file(file_name)
2     begin
3       file = File.open(file_name, "r")
4       puts file.read
5     rescue Exception => e
6       puts "An error occurred: #{e.message}"
7     ensure
8       file.close unless file.nil?
9     end
10  end
```

In this example, an attempt is made to open and read a file within a begin block. If the specified file does not exist or another error occurs during file handling, Ruby raises an Exception. The rescue block captures any Exception and prints an error message, leveraging e.message to provide the specific error information. Finally, the ensure block ensures that the file is closed, preventing resource leaks by checking that the file variable is not nil before calling file.close.

Ruby exceptions and the associated handling mechanisms are robust tools provided by the language to manage errors gracefully. By understanding and applying these constructs effectively, developers can create more reliable and maintainable Ruby applications.

7.2 Basic Exception Handling: begin, rescue, and ensure

In Ruby programming, encountering errors during the execution of a program is inevitable. To manage such situations effectively, Ruby provides a powerful mechanism known as exception handling. This section discusses the foundational constructs of Ruby's exception handling: begin, rescue, and ensure.

The begin block marks the start of a sequence of code that may potentially raise an exception. Ruby executes the code within the begin block as normal. However, if any statement raises an exception, Ruby halts the execution of the block and transfers control to the rescue block.

```
1  begin
2    # Code that might cause an exception
3    result = 10 / 0
4  rescue
5    # Code to run if an exception occurs
6    puts "Attempted to divide by zero."
7  end
```

In the example above, attempting to divide a number by zero (10 / 0) raises a ZeroDivisionError. Normally, this would cause the program to terminate abruptly. However, the presence of the rescue

161

block allows the program to handle the error gracefully, printing a message instead of crashing.

The rescue block can also be configured to catch specific types of exceptions. This is done by appending the exception class after the rescue keyword. If the raised exception matches the specified class, the corresponding rescue block is executed.

```
1   begin
2     # Code that might cause an exception
3     result = 10 / 0
4   rescue ZeroDivisionError
5     # Code to run for a ZeroDivisionError
6     puts "Attempted to divide by zero."
7   rescue StandardError => e
8     # Code to run for other types of StandardErrors
9     puts "Error occurred: #{e.message}"
10  end
```

Here, a ZeroDivisionError is explicitly rescued. Additionally, any other StandardError (a superclass of most Ruby exceptions) can be caught and handled in the second rescue block. The variable e captures the exception object, providing access to its message and other properties.

Lastly, the ensure block serves as a guarantee that certain cleanup code will run, regardless of whether an exception occurs. This is particularly useful for closing files, releasing resources, or performing other necessary finalization tasks.

```
1   begin
2     # Code that might cause an exception
3     file = File.open("example.txt")
4     # Operations on the file
5   rescue
6     puts "An error occurred while handling the file."
7   ensure
8     # This code always runs
9     file.close unless file.nil?
10    puts "File has been closed."
11  end
```

In this example, the ensure block ensures that the file is closed after being opened, irrespective of whether the operation was successful or if an exception was raised. This mechanism upholds the integrity and reliability of resource management within Ruby applications.

Through the judicious application of begin, rescue, and ensure, developers can create robust, error-resistant programs. This trio provides a structured way to handle errors gracefully, perform specific actions based on the error type, and conduct necessary cleanup, thus contributing significantly to the stability and reliability of Ruby applications.

7.3 Raising Exceptions: raise and fail Methods

In this section, we will discuss how to actively trigger exceptions in Ruby programming through the raise and fail methods. Both methods are synonymous, providing developers with the flexibility to use whichever fits their coding style or convention. Their primary function is to halt the normal execution flow of a program and raise an exception when specific conditions are met, allowing for the implementation of custom error handling logic.

To invoke an exception, the raise method is utilized in the following manner:

```
1  raise "Error message"
```

When executed, Ruby will halt the current execution with an exception, displaying the provided error message. The simplicity of this approach allows for quick and effective signaling of unexpected states or errors in program logic.

Similarly, the fail method works in the same way:

```
1  fail "Error message"
```

This method also interrupts the normal execution flow, raising an exception with a specified error message. The choice between raise and fail is purely stylistic, as they are interchangeable.

Advanced usage of raise allows specifying the exception class and a message as parameters:

```
1  raise ArgumentError, "Invalid argument"
```

In this scenario, an `ArgumentError` exception is raised, providing additional specificity about the nature of the error, facilitating more granulated exception handling.

Moreover, it is possible to raise an exception instance directly, offering even greater control over the exception's properties:

```
1  raise ArgumentError.new("Invalid argument")
```

This approach entails creating a new instance of the `ArgumentError` class explicitly, with the provided message. This method is particularly useful when working with custom exception classes, allowing for the instantiation of an exception with specific attributes or behavior.

When raising exceptions, encapsulating the logic that could potentially fail within a `begin` block, followed by one or more `rescue` blocks, ensures that the program can gracefully handle errors:

```
1  begin
2    # Code that might raise an exception
3    raise "Unexpected error"
4  rescue => error
5    puts "An error occurred: #{error.message}"
6  end
```

Here, if an exception is raised within the begin block, execution will jump to the rescue block, where the error can be logged, rectified, or communicated to the user, maintaining the robustness and reliability of the application.

In summary, the `raise` and `fail` methods are powerful tools for proactive error management in Ruby, offering a mechanism to halt execution flow and signal exceptions. Their versatility in accepting different parameters allows for detailed error reporting and precise control over application logic, ensuring that Ruby programs are both robust and maintainable.

7.4 Creating Custom Exception Classes

In this section, we will discuss how to define and use custom exception classes in Ruby. This technique allows developers to create specific types of exceptions that can handle unique error situations more effectively.

Ruby's flexible nature lets you define your own exception hierarchy, stemming from the standard Exception class. By doing so, you can significantly enhance the readability and maintainability of your error handling code, making it clearer what types of errors your application can encounter and how it deals with them.

Defining a Custom Exception Class

Defining a custom exception class in Ruby is straightforward. You simply create a new class that inherits from StandardError or one of its subclasses. Here is a basic example:

```
1  class MyCustomError < StandardError
2  end
```

This code snippet defines a new exception class called MyCustomError that inherits from StandardError. Inheritance from StandardError (rather than directly from Exception) is a best practice in Ruby since rescue blocks will only catch exceptions that are subclasses of StandardError by default.

Adding Additional Context to Your Exceptions

Often, exceptions are more useful when they can carry additional information about the error that occurred. You can achieve this by overriding the initializer of your custom exception class to accept extra arguments and storing them as instance variables. Here is an example:

```
1  class MyCustomError < StandardError
2    attr_reader :detail
3
```

165

```
4   def initialize(detail)
5     @detail = detail
6     super("An error occurred: #{detail}")
7   end
8 end
```

In this modified version of MyCustomError, the class is designed to hold a detail attribute that provides more context about the error. The super call in the initializer passes a custom message to the superclass (StandardError), which sets the exception's message. This approach not only organizes error information more effectively but also makes logs and error messages more informative and easier to debug.

Raising Custom Exceptions

Raising a custom exception is identical to raising built-in exceptions in Ruby. Use the raise keyword, followed by an instance of your custom exception class. For example:

```
1 raise MyCustomError.new("something went wrong")
```

When this code executes, Ruby raises an instance of MyCustomError with the message "An error occurred: something went wrong".

Handling custom exceptions is also similar to how you would catch standard exceptions. You can use a rescue block to catch the exception and handle it accordingly:

```
1 begin
2   # Some code that might raise MyCustomError
3 rescue MyCustomError => e
4   puts "Caught a custom error: #{e.detail}"
5 end
```

Creating custom exception classes in Ruby is a powerful technique that enhances your application's ability to handle errors gracefully and informatively. By defining classes that inherit from Ruby's exception hierarchy, you can create tailored error handling that significantly improves the debuggability and maintainability of your code.

By including additional context in your custom exceptions and using them strategically within your application, you can make your error handling code not only more expressive but also more effective at conveying the precise nature of runtime issues to developers and users alike.

7.5 Catching Exceptions with rescue Modifiers

Unlike the typical `begin-rescue-end` block, which is designed for handling exceptions in a more structured manner, the Ruby `rescue` modifier provides a shorthand for wrapping potentially risky operations. It is a succinct alternative for simple error handling scenarios where detailed exception information is not required, or the action to be taken in case of an error is relatively straightforward.

To implement a `rescue` modifier, append the `rescue` keyword followed by the code you wish to execute in the event of an exception directly after the line of code that might raise an exception. This modifier is particularly useful for inline error handling.

Consider the scenario where you are attempting to read from a file. Under normal circumstances, this operation might fail for several reasons, such as the file not existing or the program lacking the necessary permissions. Using the rescue modifier, you can address these potential issues concisely:

```
1  file_content = File.read('example.txt') rescue 'Default content'
```

In the above code snippet, if the `File.read` operation fails for any reason, Ruby will rescue the operation by returning the string `'Default content'` instead of raising an exception. This approach enables the program to continue running smoothly without interruption.

It's essential to understand that while the `rescue` modifier is a powerful tool for simplifying error handling, its usage is best limited to scenarios where the error does not require detailed examination. For complex error handling needs, where the type of exception matters or when specific actions must be taken based on the exception, a full begin-rescue-end block is more appropriate.

A point to note is that using the rescue modifier without specifying an exception class will catch all StandardError exceptions and its subclasses. It is generally a good practice to avoid rescuing all exceptions blindly unless absolutely necessary for the context. Instead, if you know the type of exceptions that may occur, you can specify them directly to make your error handling more precise:

```
1  file_content = File.read('example.txt') rescue IOError, 'Default content'
```

In this modified example, only IOError exceptions will be caught by the rescue modifier. Any other types of exceptions will not be caught and will propagate as usual. This modification makes the error handling safer and more predictable, ensuring that only expected errors are managed while unforeseen issues remain unobscured.

In summary, the rescue modifier in Ruby offers a streamlined way to handle errors inline, especially in scenarios where the error handling logic is straightforward or when the program can safely proceed with a default value or action. However, it is crucial to use this feature judiciously, considering the broader context of error management strategy in Ruby applications.

7.6   Working with the retry Statement

In error handling, Ruby's retry statement serves as a powerful tool, enabling a block of code to be attempted again after an exception has been rescued. This feature is particularly useful when dealing with operations that may fail due to transient issues, such as network timeouts or temporary resource unavailability. By judiciously applying the retry statement, developers can enhance the resilience and reliability of their applications. It is crucial, however, to employ this feature with care to avoid creating infinite loops or exacerbating performance issues.

To illustrate the use of the retry statement within a begin. . . rescue block, consider the following scenario involving a network request:

```
1   attempts = 0
2   begin
3     attempts += 1
4     # Simulating a network request that may fail
5     puts "Attempting to connect..."
6     raise "Connection error" if attempts < 3
7     puts "Connection successful!"
8   rescue => e
9     puts "Error encountered: #{e}. Retrying..."
10    retry if attempts < 3
11  end
```

In this example, a simulated network request is represented by a block of code that raises a "Connection error" exception if the number of attempts is less than 3. Upon encountering an exception, the rescue block catches it, prints an error message, and then employs the retry statement. This statement instructs Ruby to re-execute the begin block, thereby allowing another attempt at the operation. The attempts variable is incremented with each iteration, ensuring that the process is attempted a maximum of three times.

The output for this example would be as follows:

```
Attempting to connect...
Error encountered: Connection error. Retrying...
Attempting to connect...
Error encountered: Connection error. Retrying...
Attempting to connect...
Connection successful!
```

This output demonstrates the retry statement in action, with the operation being attempted three times before success is achieved.

While the retry statement offers significant benefits, it is important to approach its use with caution:

- Ensure that there is a clear exit condition to prevent infinite loops. In the given example, the number of retry attempts is capped at three.

- Consider the performance implications, especially in scenarios involving resource-intensive operations or high volumes of traffic.

- Use logging or monitoring to track the frequency and outcomes of retries, facilitating troubleshooting and performance optimization.

In summary, the retry statement in Ruby provides a mechanism for gracefully handling transient errors by attempting an operation again. When employed wisely and in appropriate contexts, it can significantly enhance the robustness of error handling in an application. However, developers must be mindful of the potential pitfalls, ensuring that retries are implemented with careful consideration of exit conditions and performance implications.

7.7   Debugging Techniques in Ruby

Debugging is a methodical process of identifying and removing bugs from software. In Ruby, several techniques and tools facilitate this process, enabling developers to efficiently track down issues and correct their code. This section discusses these techniques, including the use of built-in Ruby methods, leveraging the Ruby debugger, and employing strategic logging practices.

Built-in Ruby Methods for Debugging

Ruby includes several built-in methods that are invaluable for debugging purposes. These methods can be used to inspect variables, control flow, and understand the state of the program at various points in its execution.

puts and **p** are two commonly used methods for debugging. The **puts** method outputs a string representation of an object to the console. In contrast, **p** outputs a more detailed inspection of an object, which is often more useful for debugging complex objects.

```
1  # Example of using puts and p for debugging
2  variable = {"key" => "value"}
3  puts variable # Outputs the string representation of the object
4  p variable # Outputs a detailed inspection of the object
```

Another useful method is **pp**, which stands for "pretty print". It formats complex nested structures in a way that makes them easier to read, which is particularly useful for debugging large or deeply nested objects.

```
1  # Example of using pp for debugging
2  require 'pp'
3  complex_structure = { key1: { key2: { key3: "value" } } }
4  pp complex_structure
```

Using Ruby Debuggers: byebug and ruby-debug

For more advanced debugging, Ruby provides debugger tools such as *byebug* and *ruby-debug*. These tools allow for breakpoint management, step-by-step execution, and variable inspection, providing a powerful way to analyze and debug Ruby code.

To use *byebug*, it must first be included in the Gemfile and installed using Bundler. Once installed, the *byebug* command can be inserted into the code where debugging is needed. Execution will pause at this point, and a debugging session will start, allowing inspection and manipulation of the program's state.

```
1  # Example of using byebug for debugging
2  require 'byebug'
3
4  def problematic_method
5    byebug
6    # Code that needs debugging
7  end
```

ruby-debug operates similarly, providing a console-based interface for debugging Ruby applications. It supports setting breakpoints, stepping through code, and viewing call stacks, among other features.

Logging for Debugging and Audit Trails

Logging is an essential part of debugging, providing a way to record program execution details for later analysis. Ruby's standard library includes the Logger class, which can be used to implement logging in applications. Logs can be directed to various outputs, such as the console, file, or even over the network, and can be categorized by severity (info, warning, error, etc.).

```ruby
# Example of using Logger for debugging
require 'logger'

logger = Logger.new(STDOUT)
logger.info("Application has started")
```

Logs should contain enough context to be useful for debugging while avoiding excessive verbosity that could obscure important information. Including timestamps, unique request identifiers, and relevant variable values can greatly enhance the utility of logs for debugging purposes.

In summary, Ruby provides a range of techniques and tools to assist with debugging, from simple print statements to sophisticated debugging environments. Effectively leveraging these tools can significantly reduce the time and effort required to diagnose and fix issues in Ruby applications.

7.8 Using Ruby Debuggers: byebug and ruby-debug

Debugging is an indispensable part of software development, enabling developers to inspect the internal state of a program at specific points during its execution. Ruby, being a dynamic and expressive language, offers powerful tools for this purpose. Two of the most widely used Ruby debuggers are byebug and ruby-debug. This section aims to provide a comprehensive guide on how to effectively use these debuggers to troubleshoot and resolve issues within Ruby applications.

Installing and Setting Up byebug

byebug is a simple to use, feature-rich debugger for Ruby 2.0 and later. It allows the execution of code one line at a time, pausing execution to inspect the current environment. To get started with byebug, it must first be included in your project's Gemfile:

```
1   gem 'byebug'
```

After adding the gem, run bundle install to install byebug and make it available for use within your project.

To invoke byebug within your Ruby code, insert the following line at the point where you want the debugger to pause execution:

```
1   byebug
```

When the Ruby interpreter encounters this line, it will initiate byebug and halt, providing you with a debugging console where you can execute commands to inspect and manipulate the program's state.

Core Commands in byebug

Once inside the byebug console, various commands are at your disposal to aid in debugging. Some of the essential commands include:

- next - Moves execution to the next line in the current file, stepping over method calls.

- step - Executes the next line of code, stepping into method calls if any.

- continue - Resumes program execution until the next breakpoint or the program's end.

- break - Sets a breakpoint at a specified line or method.

- list - Displays the source code around the current line.

- var - Shows variables and their values in the current context.

Here is an example of using byebug to set a breakpoint and inspect variable values:

```
1   require 'byebug'
2
3   def compute_sum(a, b)
4     byebug
5     a + b
6   end
7
8   puts compute_sum(5, 3)
```

When executed, code execution will pause inside the `compute_sum` method, allowing the inspection and modification of the variables a and b.

ruby-debug: An Overview

ruby-debug is another potent debugger, compatible with older versions of Ruby. Its usage and commands are similar to byebug, providing a similar set of features for debugging Ruby applications.

Installation of ruby-debug is straightforward, requiring the addition of the ruby-debug gem to your Gemfile and running `bundle install`.

To initiate a debugging session using ruby-debug, insert the debugger call within your code:

```
1   require 'ruby-debug'
2   debugger
```

Although ruby-debug and byebug share many similarities, it's worth noting that byebug is more actively maintained and generally recommended for use with modern Ruby versions.

Choosing Between byebug and ruby-debug

While both byebug and ruby-debug offer powerful debugging capabilities, the choice between them largely depends on the Ruby version you are working with. For Ruby 2.0 and later, byebug is the recommended option due to its active development and compatibility. For legacy projects using older Ruby versions, ruby-debug may be the more suitable tool.

Regardless of the choice, mastering these debugging tools is crucial for efficiently diagnosing and resolving issues within Ruby applications, ultimately leading to more robust and error-free software.

7.9   Exploring the Call Stack and Variables

Understanding the call stack and variables in the context of Ruby programming is integral for efficient debugging and error handling. This section elucidates the role of the call stack in error tracking and how variables can be inspected to diagnose issues within a Ruby application.

The call stack is a record of the active subroutines or methods within a program at a given time. In Ruby, when an error occurs, the interpreter generates a call stack trace, which offers a snapshot of the method calls that led to the error. This trace is pivotal in locating the source of errors as it outlines the execution flow of the program up until the point of failure.

To comprehend the significance of the call stack, consider the following Ruby code snippet:

```
1   def method_a
2     method_b
3   end
4
5   def method_b
6     method_c
7   end
8
9   def method_c
10    raise 'An error has occurred'
11  end
12
13  method_a
```

When executed, this code will generate an error and a call stack trace that signifies the flow of execution from method_a to method_c, where the error was raised. The call stack trace serves as a roadmap for debugging, pointing to the exact line and method where the error occurred.

Besides understanding the call stack, inspecting variables' states at

various execution points is another vital aspect of debugging. Ruby
developers have several tools at their disposal for this purpose. The
p and *puts* methods can be used for simple output of variable states
to the console. However, for a more detailed inspection, one might
employ the Ruby debugger (for example, *byebug*) which allows for
setting breakpoints, stepping through code line by line, and inspecting variables' states at any point.

For instance, consider adding a breakpoint using *byebug* in the previous example:

```
1  require 'byebug'
2
3  def method_a
4    byebug
5    method_b
6  end
```

This would halt execution within `method_a`, allowing inspection of
the current execution context and variables.   Command line
debugger options such as *step* or *continue* can then be used to
navigate through the execution.

In complex Ruby applications, understanding and utilizing the call
stack, along with efficient variable inspection, can significantly ease
the debugging process. The key lies in systematically tracing back
from the point of error, using the call stack, and closely examining
the state of relevant variables to uncover the root cause of issues.

This section has highlighted the importance of the call stack and variable inspection in Ruby error handling and debugging. Mastery of
these concepts and tools enables developers to more efficiently diagnose and solve problems, leading to more stable and reliable Ruby
applications.

7.10   Logging for Debugging and Audit Trails

In the sphere of software development, the implementation of
logging is a pivotal tool for debugging and creating comprehensive
audit trails. This practice not simply aids in the detection and

diagnosis of issues post-deployment but also serves as a crucial record of the application's runtime behavior, facilitating enhanced transparency and accountability.

Logging in Ruby can be accomplished using the built-in Logger class, which provides a flexible and powerful way to record messages of varying levels of importance. Let's examine the process of setting up a basic logger, logging messages, and managing log levels.

First, initialize a logger by requiring the Logger library and creating a new Logger instance. Specify the log file path or pass STDOUT to log messages to the console.

```
1  require 'logger'
2
3  # Logging to a file
4  logger = Logger.new('logfile.log')
5
6  # Logging to the console
7  logger = Logger.new(STDOUT)
```

Once the logger is set up, you can log messages at different severity levels: DEBUG, INFO, WARN, ERROR, FATAL, and UNKNOWN. These levels allow for granular control over the output, helping to filter messages based on their importance.

```
1  logger.debug("This is a debug message")
2  logger.info("General information message")
3  logger.warn("A warning message")
4  logger.error("Error message")
5  logger.fatal("Fatal error message")
6  logger.unknown("An unknown message")
```

To dynamically control the log level, thus filtering messages at runtime, use the `logger.level` attribute. This enables or disables the logging of messages below a certain severity threshold.

```
1  # Setting the log level to DEBUG
2  logger.level = Logger::DEBUG
3
4  # Only messages at or above the DEBUG level will be logged
```

The Logger class also supports message formatting, allowing for the customization of how messages are structured in the log. This can include details such as the timestamp, severity level, program name,

177

and the actual message. Customize the format by assigning a proc to the `logger.formatter` attribute.

```
1  logger.formatter = proc do |severity, datetime, progname, msg|
2    "#{datetime}: #{severity} - #{msg}\n"
3  end
```

For creating audit trails, logging every action and transaction can prove invaluable, especially in systems where data integrity and history are critical. Ruby's Logger class can be utilized to systematically record user actions, data changes, system errors, and operational performance, thus providing a reliable mechanism for analyzing the application's behavior over time.

In summary, efficient use of logging in Ruby not only facilitates debugging by providing real-time insights into the application's state but also supports the generation of audit trails, enhancing error resolution methodologies, and ensuring a more secure and transparent application environment.

7.11   Best Practices for Error Handling and Debugging

Error handling and debugging are vital in the development of robust, stable, and efficient Ruby applications. This section is dedicated to discussing the best practices that should be followed to improve error handling and debugging processes.

- **Use Explicit Exception Handling:** Instead of allowing your Ruby application to fail randomly, employ explicit exception handling mechanisms. The use of begin, rescue, and ensure blocks allows you to capture errors gracefully and react accordingly. This practice prevents your application from crashing and provides a better user experience by handling errors more gracefully.

- **Create Meaningful Custom Exceptions:** While Ruby provides a variety of built-in exceptions, creating your own custom exception classes can help in conveying more specific error information. When raising custom exceptions, ensure that the exception names and messages are meaningful and self-explanatory, which aids in faster debugging and maintenance.

```
1  class MyCustomError < StandardError; end
2
3  raise MyCustomError, "Something specific went wrong"
```

- **Log Error Information:** Implement comprehensive logging throughout your application. Logs are essential for tracking the state of the application and are invaluable for diagnosing issues. Record as much information as possible about the error context, including error messages, stack traces, user actions, and application state.

- **Use Ruby Debugging Tools:** Familiarize yourself with Ruby's debugger tools such as byebug and ruby-debug. These tools allow you to inspect the current state of your program, evaluate expressions, and navigate through your code line by line to identify the root cause of problems.

```
1  require 'byebug'
2  byebug
3  puts "Debugging this line."
```

- **Implement Retry Mechanisms:** For operations that may fail temporarily (like network requests), implement retry mechanisms with exponential backoff. This approach can resolve transient issues without requiring intervention or crashing the program.

```
1  begin
2    # perform some network operation
3  rescue NetworkError
4    @retry_count ||= 0
5    @retry_count += 1
6    sleep(2**@retry_count)
7    retry if @retry_count < 3
8  end
```

- **Adopt a Defensive Programming Approach:** Whenever possible, anticipate and guard against potential errors by checking the validity of inputs and outputs, using assertions to validate state, and employing fail-safe defaults. This proactive approach reduces the likelihood of unhandled errors occurring.

- **Study and Learn from Errors:** Use every error as a learning opportunity. Analyze why the error occurred and what could have been done to prevent it. Over time, this practice will not only improve your current project but also enhance your overall development skills by making you more aware of potential pitfalls.

- **Regular Code Review:** Incorporate regular code reviews into your development process. Reviews by peers can identify potential issues early, suggest improvements, and share knowledge on error handling and debugging techniques. Code reviews also encourage adherence to best practices across the team.

Implementing these best practices for error handling and debugging in Ruby applications not only aids in creating more reliable and error-resistant applications but also facilitates easier maintenance and enhancements over time. These practices are essential for developers striving to enhance their skills and improve the quality of their code.

7.12 Common Ruby Errors and How to Resolve Them

In Ruby programming, certain errors are more frequently encountered than others. Understanding these common errors can significantly reduce debugging time and improve your coding efficiency. This section will discuss some of the most common Ruby errors, their causes, and strategies for resolving them.

NameError

A NameError occurs when Ruby cannot find a constant, function, or variable. It often happens due to misspelling the name of a method or variable or attempting to use a variable that has not been declared or is not in the current scope.

```
1  puts unknown_variable
```

```
NameError: undefined local variable or method `unknown_variable' for main:Object
```

To resolve a NameError, ensure that all variable and method names are spelled correctly and that any variable or method you are trying to use is defined within the current scope.

SyntaxError

A SyntaxError indicates that Ruby has encountered something unexpected in your code, often due to a missing keyword, end statement, parentheses, or brackets. This type of error can disrupt the parsing of your code and is a common issue for both beginners and experienced developers.

```
1  if x > 5
2  puts "x is greater than 5"
```

```
SyntaxError: (eval):2: syntax error, unexpected tSTRING_BEG, expecting keyword_then
    or ';' or '\n'
```

The solution to a SyntaxError is to carefully review your code for any syntax mistakes. Ensure all statements are correctly closed and that keywords are properly used.

NoMethodError

A NoMethodError occurs when calling a method on an object that does not support such a method. This error is common when

181

working with nil values or when expecting an object of a different type.

```
1  nil.split(" ")
```

```
NoMethodError: undefined method `split' for nil:NilClass
```

To resolve a NoMethodError, verify that the object on which you are calling the method exists and is of the expected type. Implement checks to ensure the object is not nil before calling methods on it or use the safe navigation operator (&.) introduced in Ruby 2.3.

TypeError

A TypeError is encountered when an operation is performed on an object of an inappropriate or unexpected type, such as attempting to add a string to an integer.

```
1  "ten" + 10
```

```
TypeError: no implicit conversion of Integer into String
```

To fix a TypeError, ensure that all operands in an operation are of compatible types. Use conversion methods like .to_s, .to_i, or .to_f to explicitly convert objects to the expected type.

ZeroDivisionError

A ZeroDivisionError occurs when attempting to divide a number by zero. Division by zero is undefined in mathematics and, consequently, in Ruby programming.

```
1  result = 10 / 0
```

```
ZeroDivisionError: divided by 0
```

To avoid a ZeroDivisionError, perform checks to ensure the denominator in a division operation is not zero before performing the division.

LoadError

A LoadError happens when Ruby cannot load an external file or library specified using require or load. This error is common when a library is not installed or the path to the file is incorrect.

```
1  require 'nonexistent_library'
```

```
LoadError: cannot load such file -- nonexistent_library
```

Resolving a LoadError typically involves installing the missing library using a package manager such as gem for Ruby or ensuring the path to the file is correct.

By understanding and being able to quickly identify these common Ruby errors, developers can significantly decrease debugging time and increase their code's robustness and reliability.

Chapter 8

Modules and Mixins

This chapter explores the concept of modules and mixins in Ruby, powerful tools for organizing code and fostering reuse without the need for traditional inheritance. It starts by explaining what modules are and how they serve as namespaces and containers for methods, constants, and class definitions. The chapter then covers how mixins allow modules to be included or extended within classes, providing a way to share functionality among disparate class hierarchies. Through practical examples, readers will learn how to use modules to keep their codebase clean, manageable, and DRY, while also understanding the intricacies of the Ruby object model as it pertains to inheritance and mixin inclusion.

8.1 Introduction to Modules: Purpose and Usage

Modules in Ruby serve a dual purpose: they function as namespaces and as a means for implementing mixins. A namespace is a container that allows programmers to group logically related entities, such as classes, methods, and constants, under a single name. This is particularly useful in avoiding name clashes between identifiers that might occur when large codebases or multiple libraries are involved.

Consider the scenario where two libraries define a class named Client. Without namespaces, Ruby would have difficulty distinguishing between the two, resulting in a conflict. By encapsulating a Client class within a module, developers can avoid this issue entirely, as illustrated below:

```
1   module LibraryA
2     class Client
3       def initialize
4         puts "Client from Library A"
5       end
6     end
7   end
8
9   module LibraryB
10    class Client
11      def initialize
12        puts "Client from Library B"
13      end
14    end
15  end
```

To instantiate a Client class from LibraryA, the following syntax is used:

```
1   client_a = LibraryA::Client.new
```

This results in the output:

```
Client from Library A
```

The use of modules as namespaces significantly enhances code clarity and prevent clashes in a multi-library environment.

Beyond serving as namespaces, modules are pivotal in the implementation of mixins. Mixins allow modules to share methods across multiple classes. Unlike class inheritance, mixins do not establish a direct parent-child relationship between classes and modules. Instead, they provide a way to share functionality horizontally across classes.

For example, consider a module called Debuggable that provides a common debug method:

```
1  module Debuggable
2    def debug
3      puts "#{self.class.name} (id: #{self.object_id}): #{self.to_s}"
4    end
5  end
```

Classes can include this module to gain its debug method without inheriting from a specific superclass:

```
1  class Widget
2    include Debuggable
3  end
4
5  class Gizmo
6    include Debuggable
7  end
```

Both Widget and Gizmo instances can now use the debug method, demonstrating how mixins facilitate code reuse in a flexible manner:

```
1  widget = Widget.new
2  widget.debug
3
4  gizmo = Gizmo.new
5  gizmo.debug
```

This code outputs the class name and object id for each instance, showcasing the debug method provided by the Debuggable module. Mixins offer a powerful mechanism for sharing functionality without the rigidity of traditional class hierarchies, promoting a more compositional design approach.

In summary, modules in Ruby are versatile constructions that provide namespaces to avoid naming conflicts and support mixins for sharing functionality across classes. This dual role makes modules an essential feature for organizing and structuring Ruby applications for clarity, maintainability, and reuse.

8.2 Defining a Ruby Module

Modules in Ruby serve a dual purpose: they offer both a namespace mechanism to avoid name clashes between different sections of code and a way to achieve polymorphism without inheritance by acting as a mix-in. They are collections of methods, constants, and class/-module definitions.

To define a Ruby module, the keyword `module` is used, followed by the module name, which must begin with a capital letter. Like class definitions, module definitions must be closed with the `end` keyword.

Consider the following example:

```
1  module Greetings
2    def say_hello
3      "Hello"
4    end
5  end
```

This module `Greetings` contains a method `say_hello` that returns the string `"Hello"`. Notice how the module encapsulates this method, making it reusable for any class that chooses to include or extend it.

Modules by themselves do not have instances. This is a key difference from classes. Attempting to create an instance of a module using the `new` keyword will result in an error:

```
NoMethodError: undefined method `new' for Greetings:Module
```

However, the real power of modules unfolds when they are used as mixins. This enables the methods defined within the module to be mixed into the class that includes or extends it, thus granting the class additional capabilities.

Let's explore an example where `Greetings` module is included in a class:

```
1  class Person
2    include Greetings
3  end
4
5  john = Person.new
6  puts john.say_hello # Output: Hello
```

By including the `Greetings` module, the `Person` class now has access to the `say_hello` method. It's worth pointing out that when a module is included using the `include` keyword, the methods defined in the module become instance methods of the class.

Alternatively, modules can also be extended. When a module is extended, its methods become class methods of the target class:

```
class Person
  extend Greetings
end

puts Person.say_hello # Output: Hello
```

The decision to include or extend a module depends on whether you want its methods to be instance methods or class methods.

Furthermore, modules can contain constants. Constants within modules can help in organizing related values together, making them easily accessible without cluttering the global namespace:

```
module Colors
  RED = '#ff0000'
  GREEN = '#00ff00'
  BLUE = '#0000ff'
end

puts Colors::RED # Output: #ff0000
```

Note the use of the double colon (::) operator to access constants within a module. This operator is used for accessing constants, instance methods, and class methods from modules or classes.

To summarize, defining a Ruby module involves the use of the `module` keyword, followed by the module's name. Modules can encapsulate methods, constants, and even other module or class definitions. They do not instantiate like classes do but are instead included or extended within classes to add additional behaviors or to serve as a namespace.

8.3 Including Modules into Classes (Mixins)

Modules in Ruby provide an elegant mechanism for sharing functionality across classes without employing traditional inheritance. Incorporating modules within classes, known as mixins, empowers developers to design flexible and maintainable codebases. This section elucidates the syntax and the underlying principles of including modules into classes, enhancing the reader's understanding through practical examples.

To include a module into a class, the Ruby keyword `include` is used directly within the class definition. When a module is included in a class, all module methods become available as instance methods in the target class. This technique is fundamentally vital for achieving polymorphism in Ruby, a language that does not support multiple inheritance.

Consider the following example of a module named `Greetable` that includes a single method, greet.

```
1  module Greetable
2    def greet
3      puts "Hello, #{name}"
4    end
5  end
```

Assume there are two classes, `Person` and `Robot`, both requiring the greet method. By including the `Greetable` module, we achieve this without duplicating the greet method code in each class.

```
1   class Person
2     include Greetable
3
4     attr_accessor :name
5
6     def initialize(name)
7       @name = name
8     end
9   end
10
11  class Robot
12    include Greetable
13
14    attr_accessor :name
15
16    def initialize(name)
17      @name = name
18    end
19  end
```

Notice in the above example, after including the `Greetable` module, both `Person` and `Robot` instances can now call the greet method, indicating the mix-in mechanism's capability to share behavior across unrelated classes.

```
person = Person.new("Alice")
person.greet
# Output: Hello, Alice

robot = Robot.new("R2-D2")
robot.greet
# Output: Hello, R2-D2
```

It's important to understand the method lookup path that Ruby utilizes to find the method to call. Upon including a module in a class, the module is inserted into the class's ancestors chain. Ruby searches this chain from left to right when resolving method calls, starting with the class itself, moving to any included modules, and finally reaching Object and BasicObject at the chain's end. This can be illustrated with the following code snippet, where the ancestors method is called on the Person class:

```
1   puts Person.ancestors
```

This would convey an array that includes the Greetable module, demonstrating its position in the lookup path:

```
[Person, Greetable, Object, Kernel, BasicObject]
```

In summary, mixins via module inclusion provide a powerful methodology for reusing code across classes in Ruby. By leveraging this feature, developers can effectively share functionality without the constraints of classical inheritance hierarchies, thus fostering more modular and adaptable code designs.

8.4   Extending Classes with Modules

Extending classes with modules represents a flexible feature of Ruby that allows classes to acquire module methods as class methods. This technique provides an elegant solution for sharing functionality without the need for multiple inheritance, which Ruby does not support. In contrast to including modules, which adds module's methods as instance methods to the class, extending a class with a module adds the module's methods directly to the class as class methods.

To elucidate this concept, consider the following Ruby code example where a module is defined and subsequently extended within a class:

```
1   module Greeter
2     def hello
3       'Hello, world!'
4     end
5   end
6
7   class MyClass
8     extend Greeter
9   end
10
11  puts MyClass.hello
```

In the example above, the `Greeter` module defines a method `hello`, which returns a greeting string. By using the `extend` keyword within `MyClass`, we are making the `hello` method available as a class method of `MyClass`. The output of the code will be:

```
Hello, world!
```

This demonstrates how modules can be extended within classes to introduce class level functionality. The `extend` keyword is crucial here as it signifies that the methods in the module should be added to the class as class methods rather than instance methods.

The flexibility of extending classes with modules becomes particularly useful in scenarios where a behavior should be available across different classes without necessarily being part of their instances. This approach adheres to the DRY (Don't Repeat Yourself) principle, as it allows for the centralization of shared behavior in modules that can then be extended across different classes.

When extending a class with a module, it is important to understand the implications on the method lookup path. Ruby has a well-defined lookup path that it follows to find where a method is defined. When a class extends a module, the methods in the module are inserted into the lookup path for class methods. To conceptualize this, consider the following visual representation using a class A extending a module B:

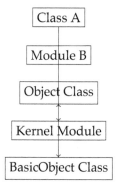

In this diagram, the arrow direction indicates the method lookup path that Ruby follows. When a class method is called on Class A, Ruby first searches within Class A itself. If the method is not found, it then searches in Module B, which has been extended by Class A. This continues down through Object Class, Kernel Module, and ultimately to BasicObject Class if necessary.

Best practices recommend being judicious with the use of module extension in classes to avoid unnecessarily complicating the method lookup path. Furthermore, clearly documenting the use of extended modules within classes is crucial for maintainability and understanding of the codebase.

In summary, extending classes with modules offers a powerful mechanism for sharing behavior across classes in Ruby. By careful application and adherence to best practices, developers can leverage this feature to write more modular, maintainable, and DRY code.

8.5 Namespace: Organizing Classes and Modules

In Ruby, the concept of a namespace is pivotal for organizing classes and modules effectively. This approach plays a critical role in preventing conflicts that may arise when classes or modules with the same name are used in a large application. A namespace operates as a container within which classes, modules, and methods can exist without colliding with others named similarly outside the container.

Creating a Namespace

To create a namespace in Ruby, one employs modules. This is accomplished by defining a module that serves purely as a container for other modules, classes, or methods. The syntax for declaring a namespace module is identical to that of any module declaration. However, its purpose is distinctly to organize and encapsulate related functional elements within its scope.

```
1  module MyApplication
2    class MyClass
3      def my_method
4        puts "Hello from MyClass within MyApplication!"
5      end
6    end
7  end
```

In this example, the MyClass class is encapsulated within the MyApplication module. Accessing this class from outside the module requires prefixing the class name with the module name, using the :: syntax, which is the namespace resolution operator in Ruby.

```
1  MyApplication::MyClass.new.my_method
```

```
Hello from MyClass within MyApplication!
```

This mechanism ensures that MyClass does not conflict with another class named MyClass that may be defined elsewhere in the application or within another library or gem.

Benefits of Using Namespaces

The use of namespaces in Ruby offers several advantages:

194

- **Avoiding Name Collisions:** As software projects grow in size and complexity, the probability of naming conflicts increases. Namespaces are instrumental in segregating symbols, reducing the likelihood of conflicts.

- **Organizing Code:** Grouping related classes and modules within a namespace simplifies the codebase structure, making it easier to understand and maintain.

- **Encapsulation:** By creating a distinct scope for code elements, namespaces aid in encapsulating the functionality, adhering to the principles of modular and object-oriented design.

- **Reusability:** Namespaces allow for greater code reuse by encapsulating functionality in a structured manner that can be easily imported and utilized in different parts of an application or across projects.

Namespaces and Module Nesting

Namespaces can also be nested within each other, providing a hierarchy of organization. This is particularly useful for further categorizing and structuring the components of a large application or library.

```
 1  module MyApplication
 2    module Admin
 3      class Dashboard
 4        def display
 5          puts "Admin Dashboard"
 6        end
 7      end
 8    end
 9  end
10
11  MyApplication::Admin::Dashboard.new.display
```

```
Admin Dashboard
```

In this scenario, the `Dashboard` class is nested within the `Admin` module, which itself resides within the `MyApplication` namespace. Such a hierarchical organization provides clarity and specificity, particularly in extensive systems where different sections or aspects of the application might need distinct categorization.

To summarize, leveraging namespaces by employing modules to encapsulate and organize related classes, modules, and methods offers a robust solution for navigating and managing the complex structure of large Ruby applications, ensuring readability, maintainability, and scalability of the codebase.

8.6   The Enumerable Module: A Deep Dive

The Enumerable module in Ruby is quintessential for performing collection-based operations. It provides a plethora of methods for traversing, searching, sorting, and manipulating collections. This module capitalizes on Ruby's internal iteration mechanism, allowing for efficient and concise code when working with arrays, hashes, and any class that includes the Enumerable module.

To include the Enumerable module in a class, one must ensure that the class defines an each method. The each method is central to the Enumerable module's functionality, as it yields successive members of the collection to the provided block. Here's an example to illustrate how a custom class can incorporate the Enumerable module by implementing an each method:

```
1   class CustomCollection
2     include Enumerable
3
4     def initialize
5       @items = []
6     end
7
8     def add(item)
9       @items << item
10    end
11
12    def each
13      @items.each { |item| yield item }
14    end
15  end
```

With the each method in place, any instance of CustomCollection now has access to Enumerable's methods such as map, select, reject, reduce, and more.

Exploring the power of the Enumerable module further, consider the map method, which allows for transformation of elements in a collection. Here's how it could be used with an instance of CustomCollection:

```
1  collection = CustomCollection.new
2  collection.add(1)
3  collection.add(2)
4  collection.add(3)
5
6  mapped_collection = collection.map { |item| item * 10 }
7
8  p mapped_collection # Output: [10, 20, 30]
```

This simplicity and elegance are what make Ruby's Enumerable module a powerful tool for manipulating collections.

Another compelling method in the Enumerable suite is reduce (also known as inject). This method is utilized to accumulate a single value by traversing through a collection. An example of calculating the sum of an array's elements using reduce is shown below:

```
1  numbers = [1, 2, 3, 4, 5]
2  sum = numbers.reduce(0) { |acc, num| acc + num }
3
4  puts sum # Output: 15
```

The reduce method takes an initial value (in this case, 0) and a block. The block is executed for each element in the collection, with acc (accumulator) holding the interim result and num representing the current element.

Understanding the Enumerable module also requires familiarity with how it interfaces with the Ruby object model, particularly concerning method lookup paths. When a class includes a module, Ruby inserts the module in the class's ancestor chain. This implies that when searching for methods, Ruby checks in the class first, then in any included modules, before finally looking in the superclass. The inclusion of the Enumerable module thus enriches a class with versatile collection manipulation capabilities without altering inheritance hierarchies.

In summary, the `Enumerable` module is indispensable in Ruby for its breadth of collection manipulation methods. Its integration with custom classes requires just an implementation of the `each` method, offering an elegant and Ruby-esque way to enhance collections with powerful, ready-to-use functionalities. Whether it's transforming elements with `map`, filtering with `select`, or accumulating values with `reduce`, the `Enumerable` module is a cornerstone of effective Ruby collection management.

8.7 The Comparable Module and Mixing in Comparison Capabilities

The Comparable module in Ruby enriches a class with comparison capabilities, allowing objects of that class to be compared using comparison operators like <, <=, ==, >, and >=. This is facilitated by the inclusion of the module and implementation of the <=> (spaceship) operator method within the class. The <=> method is expected to return -1, 0, or 1 depending on whether the left-side object is less than, equal to, or greater than the right-side object, respectively. In scenarios where the two objects are not comparable, the <=> method should return `nil`.

To incorporate the Comparable module into a class, one must follow these steps:

- Include the Comparable module inside the class definition.

- Define the <=> method within the class, ensuring it returns -1, 0, 1, or `nil` as appropriate.

Consider the following Ruby class definition for a simple `Book` object, which aims to compare books based on the number of pages they contain:

```
1  class Book
2    include Comparable
3
4    attr_reader :title, :pages
```

```
 5
 6    def initialize(title, pages)
 7      @title = title
 8      @pages = pages
 9    end
10
11    def <=>(other)
12      self.pages <=> other.pages
13    end
14  end
```

With the Comparable module included and the <=> method defined, one can now compare Book objects using the comparison operators. Here is an example that demonstrates this functionality:

```
1  book1 = Book.new("Ruby Fundamentals", 300)
2  book2 = Book.new("Advanced Ruby", 500)
3
4  puts book1 < book2
```

This code snippet would output:

```
true
```

which indicates that book1 is indeed less than book2 in terms of the number of pages.

It is essential to note that the effectiveness and efficiency of using the Comparable module depend significantly on the proper implementation of the <=> method. Incorrect or inefficient implementations may lead to unexpected behavior or performance issues when comparing objects.

In summary, the Comparable module provides a powerful yet straightforward means of adding comparison functionality to Ruby classes, with the primary requirement being the implementation of a coherent <=> method. By leveraging this module, developers can write more expressive and concise code when dealing with object comparisons.

8.8   Using Modules as a Container for Methods

Modules in Ruby provide a robust mechanism for grouping related methods together without the need to create a class. This characteristic is especially beneficial when the methods in question do not naturally fit within a specific object's scope or when there is a requirement to use them across multiple classes. By using modules as a container for methods, developers can enhance the modularity and reusability of their code.

Consider a scenario where multiple classes require access to utility methods for formatting data. Instead of duplicating these methods across classes, a module can be created to house all the related functionality.

```
# Defining a module named Formatter
module Formatter
  def format_date(date)
    date.strftime("%d-%m-%Y")
  end

  def format_currency(amount)
    sprintf("$%.2f", amount)
  end
end
```

In the above example, the Formatter module encapsulates two methods: format_date and format_currency. Neither of these methods is associated with a specific class but can be universally applied to format dates and currency values respectively.

To integrate this module within a class and utilize its methods, the include keyword is used.

```
class Report
  include Formatter
end

class Invoice
  include Formatter
end
```

With the Formatter module included in the Report and Invoice classes, instances of these classes can now directly access the format_date and format_currency methods as if they were defined within the respective class bodies.

```
1  report = Report.new
2  puts report.format_date(Date.today)
3  # Output: 23-09-2023
4
5  invoice = Invoice.new
6  puts invoice.format_currency(1550.5)
7  # Output: $1550.50
```

The code snippet demonstrates the utility of including the Formatter module within classes. It effectively extends the capabilities of the Report and Invoice classes without inheriting from another class or defining the methods redundantly in each class.

An essential characteristic of Ruby modules used as method containers is that they cannot be instantiated like classes. This feature is by design to underscore the role of modules as namespaces and providers of shared functionality rather than as entities that encapsulate data (like classes).

- Modules facilitate the DRY (Don't Repeat Yourself) principle by allowing method definitions to be written once and used in multiple places.

- The include keyword embeds module methods as instance methods in the target class.

- Modules underscore the importance of separating functionality from data structures, allowing for more flexible code design.

Utilizing modules as containers for methods offers a structured and efficient way to organize utility functions that are applicable across different classes. This approach contributes to cleaner, more manageable code and aligns with best practices in Ruby programming.

201

8.9 Module Functions: Module Methods and Instance Methods

Modules in Ruby are versatile entities that can hold a combination of methods, constants, and class definitions. Among their many uses, they serve to group logical parts of programs together, functioning as namespaces and allowing for the creation of mixins. However, a nuanced facet of modules worth exploring is their capability to define two types of method functions: module methods and instance methods. Understanding the distinction and application of these methods is crucial for structuring robust and reusable code.

Module methods, also recognized as class methods when discussed in the context of classes, are associated directly with the module itself and cannot be called on an instance of the module. To define a module method, one precedes the method definition with the module's name and a dot.

```
1   module ExampleModule
2     def self.module_method
3       "I am a module method."
4     end
5   end
6
7   puts ExampleModule.module_method
```

```
I am a module method.
```

The self keyword within the module scope refers to the module itself, making self.module_method a module method. Attempting to call this method on an instance derived from including or extending the module will result in an error, as the method is not available to the instances.

In contrast, instance methods in a module are designed to be included or extended within other classes, enabling the sharing of functionalities. When a module is included in a class, its instance methods become available to the instances of that class, whereas extending a class with a module adds the module's instance methods as class methods of the class.

```ruby
module ExampleModule
  def instance_method
    "I am an instance method."
  end
end

class MyClass
  include ExampleModule
end

obj = MyClass.new
puts obj.instance_method
```

```
I am an instance method.
```

A crucial aspect of utilizing modules effectively lies in understanding the lookup path for methods. When a module is included in a class, Ruby places the module in the inheritance chain of that class. As a result, when a method is called, Ruby searches through the class hierarchy starting from the class of the caller, moving upwards through included modules and superclasses until the method is found or an error is raised. This mechanism ensures the modular and reusable design of functionalities across different parts of a Ruby program.

The dual nature of module functions, encompassing both module and instance methods, offers a flexible framework for code organization. To facilitate the development of maintainable codebases, developers should judiciously choose between defining a method as a module method or an instance method based on the intended use case and the method's role within the system's architecture.

- Define module methods to encapsulate functionalities that are logically associated with the module itself and not with instances of classes including or extending the module.

- Utilize instance methods within modules for shared behaviors that should be available to instances of multiple class hierarchies. This is especially relevant when aiming to adhere to the DRY (Don't Repeat Yourself) principle by eliminating code redundancies.

To conclude, properly distinguishing between module methods and instance methods in modules not only enhances the clarity and organization of Ruby programs but also leverages the full potential of modules' capabilities. By strategically implementing module functions, developers can significantly improve the modularity, reusability, and maintainability of their codebases.

8.10   The Look-up Path for Methods

In this section, we will discuss the method look-up path in Ruby, which is fundamental to understanding how modules and mixins interact with the class hierarchy. When a method is called on an object, Ruby traverses a specific path to locate the method implementation. This path governs how methods are found and executed, and it plays a pivotal role when modules are included or extended within classes.

When an instance method is invoked on an object, Ruby first looks into the object's class to find the method. If the method is not found, Ruby proceeds to search within any modules included in the class. This search is conducted in the reverse order in which the modules were included, meaning the last module included is searched first. Subsequently, Ruby moves up the inheritance chain, inspecting each superclass and the modules included in them in a similar manner. This process continues until the method is either found or the search reaches the `Object` class. If the method remains unfound even in the `Object` class, a `NoMethodError` is raised.

To illustrate this concept, consider the following example:

```
1   module A
2     def method1
3       "Method in module A"
4     end
5   end
6
7   module B
8     def method2
9       "Method in module B"
10    end
11  end
12
```

```
13   class ParentClass
14     include B
15     def parent_method
16       "Method in parent class"
17     end
18   end
19
20   class ChildClass < ParentClass
21     include A
22     def child_method
23       "Method in child class"
24     end
25   end
26
27   obj = ChildClass.new
28   puts obj.method1 # Outputs: Method in module A
29   puts obj.method2 # Outputs: Method in module B
30   puts obj.parent_method # Outputs: Method in parent class
31   puts obj.child_method # Outputs: Method in child class
```

In the example, when method1 is called, Ruby's search path would be:

- ChildClass

- A (module included in ChildClass)

- ParentClass

- B (module included in ParentClass)

- Object (and upwards through the Ruby inheritance hierarchy if necessary)

This example demonstrates the method look-up path involving both superclass inheritance and mixin modules. Ruby's flexible method resolution mechanism allows for the use of mixins to inject functionality from modules in a precise and controlled manner, enhancing the reusability and modular design of Ruby applications.

Moreover, when a module is *extended* in a class, its methods become class methods of the target class. The look-up path for class methods mirrors that of instance methods, with the difference that the search starts with the singleton class of the object (which in the case of class methods is the class itself).

Understanding the method look-up path is crucial for debugging and designing Ruby applications, particularly when dealing with complex class hierarchies or involving multiple mixins. By mastering this concept, developers can effectively navigate and manipulate Ruby's object model to achieve clean, maintainable, and DRY code.

8.11   Avoiding   Name   Clashes   with Namespacing

Namespacing in Ruby provides a systematic way of encapsulating classes, modules, and methods to prevent conflicts arising from naming similarities. It is a crucial feature, particularly in large applications or when incorporating third-party libraries, where the probability of name collisions increases significantly. Through namespacing, Ruby ensures that each identifier's scope is maintained within its contextual boundary, allowing for the same name to be used in different contexts without interference.

Let's delve into the mechanics of namespacing in Ruby, with particular attention to modules as the primary mechanism for achieving this.

First, consider a scenario where two libraries are being used in a Ruby application, and both define a class named Client. Without namespacing, Ruby would only be able to reference the last Client class defined, leading to potential errors or unexpected behavior. Namespacing allows each Client class to coexist by providing a unique module as a container for each.

```
1   module LibraryA
2     class Client
3       def initialize
4         puts "Client from Library A"
5       end
6     end
7   end
8
9   module LibraryB
10    class Client
11      def initialize
```

```
12        puts "Client from Library B"
13     end
14   end
15 end
```

In this example, the `Client` class is encapsulated within `LibraryA` and `LibraryB` modules, creating distinct namespaces. To instantiate a client from Library A:

```
1 client_a = LibraryA::Client.new
```

Similarly, to instantiate a client from Library B:

```
1 client_b = LibraryB::Client.new
```

The `::` is a scope resolution operator that navigates the namespaces to locate the `Client` class within the appropriate module. This is how Ruby disambiguates between identically named classes.

Benefits of Using Namespaces

Employing namespaces in Ruby provides several benefits:

- **Clarity and Organization:** Namespaces logically group related classes and modules, making the codebase easier to navigate and understand.

- **Reduced Collision Risk:** By segregating identifiers into different namespaces, the risk of name collisions is significantly minimized.

- **Enhanced Modularity:** Namespaces facilitate modular design by allowing the same name to be reused in different contexts without conflict.

Best Practices for Namespacing

When leveraging namespaces in Ruby, consider the following best practices:

- Use descriptive names for modules to clearly indicate the scope and purpose of the encapsulated identifiers.

- Avoid deeply nested namespaces, as they can complicate the code structure and make it difficult to understand.

- When incorporating external libraries, always inspect their namespacing to avoid conflicts with your application's identifiers.

Namespacing is a powerful feature in Ruby that aids in organizing code, avoiding naming clashes, and promoting cleaner, more modular designs. By adhering to best practices and employing namespaces judiciously, developers can significantly enhance the maintainability and clarity of their Ruby applications.

8.12   Best Practices for Organizing with Modules and Mixins

Organizing code in a manageable, maintainable, and reusable fashion is fundamental in software development. Modules and mixins in Ruby offer powerful mechanisms towards accomplishing this goal. However, applying these tools effectively requires adherence to certain best practices.

Meaningful Module and Mixin Names

Choose descriptive names for modules and mixins that clearly reflect their functionality. This enhances code readability and maintainability. Consider the purpose of the module or mixin and let this inform its name. For instance, a module providing authentication features could be named `Authenticatable`.

Keep Modules Focused

Modules should adhere to the Single Responsibility Principle, meaning they should only represent one concern or functionality. This practice ensures that modules remain reusable and easy to understand. Split large modules that serve multiple purposes into smaller, more focused modules.

Leverage Namespacing

Use namespacing to group related classes and modules, which helps avoid name clashes and keeps the structure of your codebase clear. For example, if developing a payment processing system, one might organize classes and modules under a Payments namespace. This can be achieved as follows:

```ruby
module Payments
  class Invoice
    # Invoice related methods here
  end

  class Refund
    # Refund related methods here
  end
end
```

This approach makes the organizational structure of the codebase easy to understand and navigate.

Use Mixins Judiciously

While mixins are a powerful feature for sharing functionality across classes, they should be used judiciously. Overuse of mixins can make the class hierarchy and method lookup path complex and difficult to understand. Ensure that the functionality being mixed into a class is genuinely shared across multiple classes rather than being used to inject functionality into a single class.

Documenting Modules and Mixins

Provide comprehensive documentation for each module and mixin, explaining its purpose, usage, and any assumptions it makes about the environment it operates in. This is especially important for mixins that are designed to be included in multiple classes. Documentation should also cover any methods that classes need to implement to properly use the mixin.

```ruby
module Authenticatable
  # This module provides authentication features.
  # Classes including this module need to implement `find_by_credentials` method.

  def login(username, password)
    user = find_by_credentials(username, password)
    # login logic here
  end
end
```

Testing Modules and Mixins

Ensure that all modules and mixins are thoroughly tested, both in isolation and when included or extended in classes. Use unit tests to verify the functionality of methods within the module or mixin. Additionally, write integration tests for classes that include or extend these modules to ensure they behave as expected in the context of the full application.

Avoid Mixing In Methods With Side Effects

When including or extending modules, be cautious of mixing in methods that might have unintended side-effects on the class or module. Methods in mixins should ideally be pure functions, relying only on their input parameters to produce output, and not on the state of the class they are mixed into unless explicitly designed to do so.

Following these best practices will help developers leverage the full power of Ruby's modules and mixins, leading to a codebase that is both more manageable and maintainable. By organizing code logically, documenting thoroughly, testing rigorously, and using mixins judiciously, developers can create robust, reusable code structures that stand the test of time.

Chapter 9

Input and Output in Ruby

This chapter covers the essential aspects of input and output (I/O) in Ruby, providing readers with the knowledge needed to interact with the file system, external data sources, and the user. It discusses how to read from and write to files, manipulate file pointers, and perform file querying operations. The chapter also explores working with directories, handling standard input, output, and error streams, and utilizing command line arguments. Through understanding Ruby's I/O capabilities, developers will be equipped to build applications that can effectively communicate with the outside world, process data, and respond to user input.

9.1   Understanding I/O Streams in Ruby

In Ruby, I/O streams are fundamental to performing input and output operations. An I/O stream represents a continuous flow of data between a source or destination and your program. Ruby abstracts the complexities of these operations, offering an intuitive interface for handling files, standard inputs, and outputs, among others.

Overview of I/O Streams

At its core, Ruby categorizes I/O streams into two main types: input streams and output streams. Input streams are used for reading data into a program, while output streams are used for writing data from a program.

Standard I/O Streams

Ruby automatically provides three standard streams:

- Standard Input (STDIN): This is the default input stream, typically associated with keyboard input.

- Standard Output (STDOUT): This stream is used for normal output from the program. By default, it is linked to the console.

- Standard Error (STDERR): This stream handles error or warning messages. It is also directed to the console in a standard setup.

Interacting with I/O Streams

Interacting with I/O Streams in Ruby is streamlined to enhance developer productivity. Here are some fundamentals:

Reading from STDIN:
Reading user input from the command line can be achieved through methods like gets or readline. They listen for user input until the "Enter" key is pressed.

```
1  puts "Enter your name:"
2  name = gets.chomp
3  puts "Hello, #{name}!"
```

The chomp method is used here to remove the newline character that gets appends to the input string.

Writing to STDOUT and STDERR:
Outputting data to the console can be done using puts or print

methods. To write an error message to STDERR, the warn method can be utilized.

```
1  puts "This is a standard output message."
2  warn "This is an error message."
```

Redirecting Streams

Stream redirection is a powerful feature allowing the rerouting of input and output streams to or from files or other streams.

Redirecting STDOUT to a file can be performed by opening a file in write mode and assigning it to $stdout:

```
1  $stdout = File.open("output.txt", "w")
2  puts "This will be written to output.txt"
```

Upon executing the above snippet, the message "This will be written to output.txt" will not appear on the console but will be found in the "output.txt" file.

In summary, understanding and effectively utilizing I/O streams in Ruby can significantly augment a program's ability to interact with the surrounding environment. By mastering standard streams and stream manipulation, developers can create applications that seamlessly process input and output data.

9.2 Reading from and Writing to Files

Interacting with files is a fundamental part of programming, allowing applications to persist data across sessions, communicate with other processes, and manage configuration and log data. Ruby simplifies file manipulation through a cohesive and easy-to-understand API. This section details the methods and practices for efficiently reading from and writing to files in Ruby.

Opening a File

Ruby uses the `File.open` method to access a file. This method can operate in different modes, such as read-only (`"r"`), write-only (`"w"`), or appending (`"a"`). When opening a file for writing or appending, a new file is created if it does not exist. The `File.open` method can be used with a block, ensuring that the file is closed after the block's execution.

```
File.open('example.txt', 'r') do |file|
  puts file.read
end
```

Reading from a File

To read content from a file, Ruby offers several methods like `read`, `readline`, and `readlines`. The `read` method can read the entire file content as a string, while `readline` reads a single line at a time. The `readlines` method returns an array containing all lines in the file.

```
# Reading the entire file
content = File.read('example.txt')
puts content

# Reading line by line
File.open('example.txt', 'r') do |file|
  file.each_line do |line|
    puts line
  end
end
```

Writing to a File

Writing to a file in Ruby is straightforward with the use of `write` and `puts`. The `write` method writes data to a file without adding a newline at the end, unlike `puts` which appends a newline after the content.

```
File.open('output.txt', 'w') do |file|
  file.write("Hello, Ruby!\n")
  file.puts "Another line."
end
```

Appending to a File

Appending to a file rather than overwriting its content is done by opening the file in append mode (`"a"`). This ensures that new data is added to the end of the file.

```
1  File.open('example.txt', 'a') do |file|
2    file.puts "Appended line."
3  end
```

Closing the File

While the block form of `File.open` automatically closes the file after block execution, files opened without a block must be closed manually using `file.close`. It is essential to close files to free up system resources.

```
1  file = File.open('example.txt', 'r')
2  # Perform file operations
3  file.close
```

Utilizing these methods and practices, developers can effectively manage file operations in Ruby, thus enabling robust data handling capabilities for applications.

9.3 File Manipulation: Opening, Reading, Writing, and Closing

File manipulation is a fundamental aspect of Ruby programming, allowing developers to create, access, modify, and delete files within their applications. This section delves into the operations of opening, reading from, writing to, and closing files in Ruby, elucidating each step with comprehensible examples.

Opening Files

To work with files in Ruby, the first step is to open the file using the
File.open method. This method requires at least one argument: the
path to the file. Optionally, it can also take a second argument specifying the mode—such as read, write, or append mode.

```
1  file = File.open("example.txt", "r")
```

This code snippet opens example.txt in read mode ("r"). If the file
does not exist, Ruby will raise an Errno::ENOENT exception.

Reading from Files

Once a file is opened in read mode, you can read its content in several
ways: reading the entire file at once, reading it line by line, or reading
a specific amount of characters.

Reading Entire File

```
1  content = file.read
2  puts content
```

This will read the entire content of example.txt and store it in the
variable content.

Reading Line by Line

```
1  file.each do |line|
2    puts line
3  end
```

This iterates over each line in the file, printing it to the console.

Reading a Specific Number of Characters

```
1  content = file.read(10)
2  puts content
```

This reads the first 10 characters from the file.

Writing to Files

To write to a file, it must be opened in write ("w") or append ("a") mode. Write mode overwrites the entire file, while append mode adds to the end of the file.

```
1  File.open("example.txt", "w") do |file|
2    file.write("Hello, Ruby!")
3  end
```

This snippet opens example.txt in write mode and inserts the text "Hello, Ruby!".

Closing Files

It is crucial to close a file after operations are completed to free up system resources. Ruby provides the File.close method for this purpose.

```
1  file.close
```

Alternatively, when using a block with File.open, Ruby automatically closes the file at the end of the block, making explicit closure unnecessary.

Best Practices

- Always close files explicitly unless using a block with File.open.

- Handle exceptions, such as attempting to read from or write to a file that doesn't exist.

- Prefer block syntax with File.open for better resource management.

- Be cautious with file modes, especially when writing, to avoid unintentionally overwriting important data.

Understanding and implementing these file manipulation operations equip developers with the tools to manage file-related tasks, crucial for many Ruby applications that interact with the file system.

9.4   Working with Directories

Working with directories in Ruby is straightforward yet powerful. Ruby provides several methods that allow programmers to perform directory creation, deletion, navigation, and interrogation tasks efficiently. This section will discuss how to utilize these methods to manage directories.

To begin, creating a new directory can be accomplished using the `Dir.mkdir` method. This method takes a string argument representing the path of the new directory. Optionally, it allows for setting permissions on the newly created directory.

```
1  Dir.mkdir("new_directory")
```

Deleting a directory is just as simple, using the `Dir.delete` or `Dir.rmdir` methods. Both methods are synonymous and will remove an empty directory specified by its path.

```
1  Dir.delete("old_directory")
```

Navigating the file system involves changing the current working directory. Ruby enables this through the `Dir.chdir` method. Passing a directory path to `Dir.chdir` switches the current working directory to the specified path.

```
1  Dir.chdir("/path/to/directory")
```

Listing the contents of a directory is a common operation. This can be performed using the `Dir.entries` method, which returns an array containing the names of all files and directories within the specified directory.

```
1   entries = Dir.entries("/path/to/directory")
2   \end{verbatim}
3
4   Inspecting the list of entries can reveal the structure of the directory's
        contents:
5
6   \begin{verbatim}
7   puts entries
8   \end{verbatim}
9
10  Ruby also provides a convenient way to iterate over the contents of a directory
        using the \texttt{Dir.each} method. This method accepts a block, executing
        the block for each entry found in the directory.
11
12  \begin{lstlisting}
13  Dir.each("/path/to/directory") do |entry|
14    puts entry
15  end
```

For more complex directory traversal needs, Ruby offers the Find module. This module's Find.find method can recursively visit all files and directories beneath a specified directory.

```
1   require 'find'
2
3   Find.find("/path/to/directory") do |path|
4     puts path
5   end
```

In addition to these operations, Ruby allows querying properties of directories using various File class methods, due to directories being a special kind of file. For example, checking if a specific path is a directory can be done using File.directory?.

```
1   if File.directory?("/path/to/directory")
2     puts "This is a directory."
3   else
4     puts "This is not a directory."
5   end
```

This concludes the overview of working with directories in Ruby. By leveraging Ruby's directory manipulation methods, developers can create scripts that intelligently interact with the file system, performing tasks like automated housekeeping, file organization, or data retrieval operations.

9.5 Standard Input, Output, and Error Streams

The interaction between Ruby programs and their environment can be facilitated through standard streams, specifically standard input (stdin), standard output (stdout), and standard error (stderr). These streams represent channels through which data flows into and out of a program, enabling it to communicate with the operating system, users, and other programs. This section will elucidate the operations associated with these streams.

Standard Input (stdin)

Standard input is a stream from which a Ruby program reads its input. This typically originates from the keyboard but can also be redirected from a file or another program. To read input from stdin, Ruby provides the gets method. This method reads a line from stdin including the newline character, which can be removed using the chomp method.

```
1  puts "Enter your name:"
2  name = gets.chomp
3  puts "Hello, #{name}!"
```

In this example, gets reads the input from the user, and chomp removes the newline character at the end of the input. puts then prints a greeting message to the standard output.

Standard Output (stdout)

Standard output is where a Ruby program sends its output. This is typically to the console, but like stdin, it can be redirected to a file or another program. Ruby uses methods such as print and puts for writing to stdout.

```
1  print "This will be printed "
2  puts "and so will this, with a newline."
```

print outputs the string exactly as is, while puts adds a newline to the end of the output. Both write to stdout.

Standard Error (stderr)

Standard error is a separate stream used for outputting error messages or diagnostics. It allows error messages to be directed separately from regular output, which can be useful for debugging or when outputting the results to a file.

```
1  $stderr.puts "Error: Something went wrong."
```

This snippet demonstrates writing an error message to stderr using $stderr.puts. While the content appears on the console by default, stderr can be redirected independently of stdout.

Redirecting Streams

Ruby and the operating system allow for the redirection of these streams. For example, a file can serve as stdin or capture the output of stdout and stderr.

```
$ ruby myscript.rb < input.txt > output.txt 2> error.log
```

This command line snippet demonstrates redirecting stdin to read from *input.txt*, stdout to write to *output.txt*, and stderr to write to *error.log*.

To conclude, understanding and manipulating the standard input, output, and error streams is fundamental for Ruby developers, empowering them to control data flow and communicate more effectively within their programs and with the external environment.

9.6   Using   ARGV   for   Command   Line   Arguments

Command line arguments are an invaluable tool in Ruby, providing a straightforward method for passing data into a script at runtime. Ruby employs the ARGV array to store these command line arguments, which can be manipulated just as any other array in Ruby. Understanding how to utilize ARGV can significantly enhance the versatility and usability of Ruby scripts, allowing for dynamic input that can adjust the script's operation based on user-supplied information.

ARGV is a global array, available throughout your Ruby script once it starts execution. Each element of ARGV is a string corresponding to the arguments passed from the command line, in the order they are provided. Consider the following example:

```
1  # hello.rb
2  puts "Hello, #{ARGV[0]}!"
```

If you were to execute this script from the command line as follows:

```
ruby hello.rb World
```

The output would be:

```
Hello, World!
```

In this case, ARGV[0] contains the string "World", demonstrating how command line arguments can be accessed within a Ruby script.

Iterating over ARGV

It is often useful to process multiple command line arguments. Ruby's array methods can be applied to ARGV to iterate over each argument. For example:

```
1   # print_args.rb
2   ARGV.each do |arg|
3     puts arg
4   end
```

Executing this script with multiple arguments:

```
ruby print_args.rb foo bar baz
```

Would produce:

```
foo
bar
baz
```

Each argument passed to the script is printed on its own line, show-casing how ARGV can be used in conjunction with Ruby's array iteration methods.

Managing non-string arguments

While ARGV treats all command line arguments as strings, often scripts require numerical inputs. Ruby provides methods to convert string representations of numbers to their respective numeric types. For example:

```
1   # add.rb
2   sum = ARGV[0].to_i + ARGV[1].to_i
3   puts "The sum is: #{sum}"
```

This script, when run with numerical arguments, will output their sum:

```
ruby add.rb 5 7
```

Would yield:

```
The sum is: 12
```

This demonstrates converting command line arguments from strings (`ARGV` elements) to integers using the `to_i` method, enabling numerical operations on input values.

It is crucial to ensure that scripts gracefully handle scenarios where the expected arguments are not provided or are not in the expected format. Robust error handling and input validation mechanisms can improve the reliability and user-friendliness of your Ruby scripts significantly.

Limitations and Precautions

While `ARGV` provides a powerful mechanism for accepting command line input, it is essential to consider security implications, especially when handling inputs that might affect the execution flow or data integrity of the script. Always validate and sanitize user inputs to safeguard against potential security vulnerabilities, such as injection attacks or unintended operations.

Effectively using `ARGV` in Ruby scripts allows developers to write more dynamic, flexible, and interactive programs. By understanding and implementing the techniques discussed, from basic argument access and iteration to input conversion and validation, you can harness the full potential of command line argument processing in your Ruby applications.

9.7   File I/O with External Encoding

Understanding and managing the encoding of files in Ruby is critical for developers working with internationalization or dealing with files originating from various systems. Ruby provides robust support for handling external encodings, enabling developers to read from and write to files using specific character sets.

When opening a file for reading or writing, Ruby allows for the specification of an external encoding. This is accomplished through the `encoding` option in the file open method. The format for specifying encoding is "external:internal", where external is the encoding of the read or written file, and internal is the encoding used within the Ruby script. If the internal encoding is omitted, Ruby assumes it to be the same as the external encoding.

```
1   File.open('example.txt', 'r:UTF-8') do |file|
2     contents = file.read
3     puts contents
4   end
```

In the example above, the file example.txt is opened with UTF-8 encoding for reading. Ruby reads the file's contents into the variable contents using UTF-8 encoding and then prints it to the console.

It is also possible to convert the encoding of a file's contents as it is read into a Ruby script. This is done by specifying both the external and internal encodings.

```
1   File.open('example.txt', 'r:ISO-8859-1:UTF-8') do |file|
2     contents = file.read
3     puts contents.encode('UTF-8')
4   end
```

In this case, the file is read using ISO-8859-1 encoding, but its contents are converted to UTF-8 encoding as they are read into the Ruby script. The encode method explicitly ensures that the output is in UTF-8, even though this may be redundant due to the internal encoding setting.

When writing to files, specifying the encoding ensures that the data is correctly encoded as it is written to disk.

```
1   File.open('example_output.txt', 'w:UTF-8') do |file|
2     file.write("Some sample text with UTF-8 encoding.")
3   end
```

This snippet writes a string to example_output.txt using UTF-8 encoding. The 'w:UTF-8' argument in the File.open method call indicates that the file is opened for writing with UTF-8 encoding.

- It is essential to specify the correct encoding when interfacing with files to prevent data corruption or character misrepresentation.

- Ruby's   default   external   encoding   is
  Encoding.default_external, which can be set to change the
  default encoding for all file operations.

- Using the incorrect encoding can lead to errors or unexpected
  behavior when processing file contents.

Handling external encoding is particularly important in applications
dealing with multinational datasets, web scraping, or legacy systems.
By leveraging Ruby's encoding capabilities, developers can ensure
that their applications are robust, flexible, and capable of managing
diverse data sources efficiently.

9.8   Serializing and Deserializing Objects with YAML and JSON

Serialization is the process of converting an object into a format that
can be easily stored or transmitted, and subsequently reconstructed.
In Ruby, two of the most common formats for serialization are YAML
(YAML Ain't Markup Language) and JSON (JavaScript Object Notation). This section will discuss how to serialize and deserialize Ruby
objects using these formats, enabling the storage of complex objects
in text files or their transmission over networks.

Serialization with YAML

YAML is a human-readable data serialization format.   It is
particularly suited for configuration files, log files, and in
applications where data is being stored or transmitted.

To serialize an object to YAML in Ruby, the YAML module is used,
which is part of the Ruby standard library.   The first step is to
require the yaml library:

```
1  require 'yaml'
```

228

After including the YAML library, any Ruby object can be serialized using the to_yaml method. For example, to serialize a simple hash object:

```
1  person = { name: 'John Doe', age: 30 }
2  yaml_data = person.to_yaml
3  puts yaml_data
```

The output in YAML format will be:

```
---
:name: John Doe
:age: 30
```

To deserialize YAML data back into a Ruby object, the YAML.load method is used:

```
1  deserialized_person = YAML.load(yaml_data)
2  puts deserialized_person # => {:name=>"John Doe", :age=>30}
```

Serialization with JSON

JSON is a lightweight data-interchange format. It is easy for humans to read and write and for machines to parse and generate. JSON is language-agnostic, making it an ideal format for data interchange.

Ruby's standard library includes the json library for parsing and generating JSON. To use it, the library must first be required:

```
1  require 'json'
```

To serialize a Ruby object into JSON, the to_json method is utilized:

```
1  person = { name: "John Doe", age: 30 }
2  json_data = person.to_json
3  puts json_data
```

The JSON representation of the person hash will be:

```
{"name":"John Doe","age":30}
```

Deserialization from JSON back to a Ruby object is accomplished using the JSON.parse method:

```
1   deserialized_person = JSON.parse(json_data)
2   puts deserialized_person # => {"name"=>"John Doe", "age"=>30}
```

Both YAML and JSON provide powerful means for serializing and deserializing Ruby objects. The choice between them depends on the specific requirements of the application, such as the need for human readability, language interoperability, or data size.

In addition to basic serialization and deserialization, both the YAML and JSON libraries offer a range of features for customizing the process, such as symbolizing keys on deserialization or controlling the formatting of serialized data. Mastering these techniques will enable Ruby developers to efficiently store, transmit, and manipulate complex data structures, enhancing the capability and flexibility of their applications.

Best Practices

When working with serialization and deserialization in Ruby, it's important to follow best practices to ensure data integrity and security:

- Always validate and sanitize input when deserializing data from untrusted sources to prevent attacks such as code injection.

- Use the Oj (Optimized JSON) gem for improved performance when dealing with large JSON data sets.

- Leverage Ruby's built-in methods for symbols and objects to ensure accurate data conversion between formats.

- Ensure that any serialized data destined for storage or transmission is properly encoded to match the expected character set of the medium.

By adhering to these guidelines, developers can safely and efficiently incorporate serialization and deserialization into their Ruby applications.

9.9   Executing   External   Commands   from Ruby Scripts

Executing external commands from within a Ruby script enables the integration of system utilities and third-party applications directly into Ruby programs. This can significantly enhance the functionality and flexibility of Ruby scripts, allowing them to perform a wide range of tasks that extend beyond the capabilities of Ruby itself. In this section, three primary techniques for executing external commands are discussed: using backticks, the `system` method, and the `exec` command.

Using Backticks

The simplest way to execute an external command in Ruby is by enclosing the command within backticks (``` `` ```). This method captures the output of the command as a string, which can then be utilized within the Ruby script.

```
1  output = `ls`
2  puts output
```

The above example executes the `ls` command, which lists the contents of the current directory. The output of this command is stored in the variable `output`.

The System Method

The `system` method offers a more robust way of executing external commands by providing direct access to the command line. Unlike the backticks method, `system` does not capture the output of the command. Instead, it returns `true` if the command was executed successfully and `false` otherwise.

```
1  success = system('ls')
2  if success
3    puts 'Command executed successfully'
4  else
```

```
5    puts 'Command execution failed'
6  end
```

The Exec Command

The exec command is used when it is necessary to replace the current process with the external command entirely. This means that any code following an exec command within the script will not be executed.

```
1  exec('ls')
2  puts 'This line will never be executed'
```

Choosing the Right Method

The choice of method depends on the specific requirements of the task at hand. If capturing the output of the command is necessary, using backticks is the simplest solution. For tasks that require checking the success or failure of a command without needing its output, the system method is more appropriate. Finally, in situations where the Ruby script's sole purpose is to execute an external command, exec provides a clean and efficient way to achieve this.

It is also possible to capture both the output and the exit status of a command by using Open3.capture3, which is part of Ruby's Open3 library. This method is beyond the scope of this section but is worth exploring for more complex needs.

In summary, Ruby provides several methods for executing external commands, each with its use cases and benefits. By understanding these methods, developers can choose the most appropriate one for their needs, allowing for the creation of powerful and flexible Ruby applications.

9.10 Redirecting Output and Capturing Errors

In Ruby programming, effectively managing the output of your programs as well as capturing any errors that may occur during execution are crucial capabilities. This enables developers to create robust applications that can handle unexpected situations gracefully and maintain a log of important events for troubleshooting. This section delves into the mechanisms Ruby provides for redirecting standard output (stdout) and standard error (stderr), alongside practical examples to illustrate their applications.

To redirect stdout or stderr in Ruby, one might opt to overwrite these global variables ($stdout and $stderr) with instances of the File class, pointing to a different output destination. This technique is useful for logging or diverting output to a file for later analysis.

```
1  # Redirecting stdout to a file
2  $stdout = File.new('log.txt', 'w')
3  puts "This will be written to log.txt instead of the console."
4
5  # Restoring stdout to its original state
6  $stdout = STDOUT
```

Similarly, to capture errors and redirect them to a file or another output stream:

```
1  # Redirecting stderr to a file
2  $stderr = File.new('errors.log', 'w')
3  warn "This error message will go to errors.log instead of stderr."
4
5  # Restoring stderr to its original state
6  $stderr = STDERR
```

In addition to rerouting stdout and stderr, Ruby provides a sophisticated way of handling exceptions and capturing error messages through the use of *begin-rescue-end* blocks. This allows for specific error handling and redirection of error messages as needed.

```
1  begin
2    # Code that might cause an error
3    raise "An error occurred."
4  rescue => error
5    File.open('errors.log', 'a') {|f| f.puts error.message }
```

```
6  end
```

The above snippet demonstrates capturing an exception and appending its message to an 'errors.log' file. This is particularly useful for maintaining a history of errors that an application encounters during its execution, providing valuable insights for debugging.

For complex Ruby applications, especially those running in production environments, it's often necessary to capture both standard output and errors simultaneously to monitor the application's health and debug issues efficiently. This can be achieved by redirecting both streams to the same log file or to different logs, depending on the requirements.

An advanced technique involves the use of Ruby's Open3 library for executing external commands while capturing their stdout, stderr, and exit status. This is especially useful for interacting with the operating system or other command-line tools within a Ruby script.

```
1  require 'open3'
2
3  stdout, stderr, status = Open3.capture3('ls non_existent_directory')
4  puts "stdout is: #{stdout}"
5  puts "stderr is: #{stderr}"
6  puts "exit status: #{status.exitstatus}"
```

```
stdout is:
stderr is: ls: non_existent_directory: No such file or directory
exit status: 1
```

As demonstrated, Open3.capture3 method facilitates the execution of a command while capturing its stdout, stderr, and exit status, which are invaluable for debugging and ensuring the resilience of Ruby applications.

Mastering the redirection of output and capturing errors in Ruby empowers developers to build highly reliable applications with enhanced debugging capabilities. Through the use of global variables for stream redirection, exception handling mechanisms, and the Open3 library, Ruby offers a comprehensive set of tools for effective output management and error logging.

9.11   Networking: Sockets and Web Requests

Ruby provides several classes within its standard library to facilitate networking and web requests. This capability enables Ruby applications to send and receive data over the internet, interact with web services, and perform network communication. Two critical aspects of Ruby's networking capabilities are socket programming and executing web requests.

Socket Programming in Ruby

Sockets are the endpoints of a bidirectional communication channel used for network communication between two processes on the same or different machines. Ruby's Socket class provides a comprehensive suite of methods to work with sockets.

- To create a socket, you typically start by initializing a new Socket object, specifying the address family, socket type, and protocol.

- After creation, the socket is then bound to a network address and port using the bind method.

- For a server socket, you would call listen to start listening for incoming connections and accept to accept these connections.

- Data is sent and received using the send and recv methods, respectively.

Below is a simple example of a TCP server and client in Ruby using sockets:

```
1  # TCP Server Example
2  require 'socket'
3  server = TCPServer.new(5678)
4  while session = server.accept
5      session.puts "Hello World!"
6      session.close
7  end
```

```
1  # TCP Client Example
2  require 'socket'
3  socket = TCPSocket.new('localhost', 5678)
4  puts socket.gets
5  socket.close
```

Web Requests using Net::HTTP

For higher-level network communications, such as HTTP requests, Ruby offers the Net::HTTP class. It simplifies the process of interacting with web services.

- The Net::HTTP class supports various HTTP methods like GET, POST, PUT, and DELETE.

- A simple web request can be made by creating a new instance of Net::HTTP, specifying the target URI, and then invoking the corresponding method for the desired HTTP request.

Below is an example demonstrating how to make a GET request to a web service:

```
1  require 'net/http'
2  require 'uri'
3
4  uri = URI.parse("http://example.com/")
5  response = Net::HTTP.get_response(uri)
6
7  puts response.body
```

This code snippet will fetch the content of http://example.com/ and print it to the console.

Error Handling

Both socket programming and web requests are susceptible to various errors, such as connection timeouts, unreachable hosts, or invalid responses. It is crucial to implement error handling mechanisms to manage such situations gracefully. Ruby's standard error handling approach using `begin`, `rescue`, and `ensure` blocks is applicable in networking scenarios to catch exceptions and perform necessary cleanup operations.

In summary, Ruby's networking capabilities, through socket programming and the `Net::HTTP` class, facilitate both low-level and high-level network communications. By leveraging these features, developers can build robust Ruby applications capable of interacting with other systems over the network efficiently.

9.12 Best Practices for I/O Operations

In the context of Input/Output operations within Ruby, adhering to a set of best practices ensures robust, efficient, and secure code execution. This section delineates these practices, providing a guide to optimize I/O operations.

- **Use Block Syntax with Files:** When dealing with file operations, employing the block syntax is recommended. This approach automatically closes the file once operations within the block are completed, thus preventing potential file leaks.

```
1  File.open('example.txt', 'r') do |file|
2    puts file.read
3  end
```

- **Handle Exceptions:** I/O operations are prone to errors such as file not found, permissions issues, or device errors. Encapsulating I/O instructions within a `begin-rescue-end` block assists in managing exceptions effectively.

```
1  begin
2    File.foreach('nonexistent.txt') do |line|
3      puts line
4    end
5  rescue Exception => e
6    puts "An error occurred: #{e.message}"
7  end
```

- **Prefer IO#binread and IO#binwrite for Binary Files:** When working with binary files, using IO#binread and IO#binwrite ensures that data is read or written in binary mode, preserving the file's integrity.

```
1  binary_data = IO.binread('image.png')
2  IO.binwrite('copy.png', binary_data)
```

- **Utilize String#encode for External Encoding:** When reading from or writing to files with different encodings, use the String#encode method to convert between encodings, preventing data corruption.

```
1  content = File.read('example.txt')
2  encoded_content = content.encode('UTF-8', 'ISO-8859-1')
3  File.write('encoded_example.txt', encoded_content)
```

- **Be Aware of Buffered I/O:** Ruby employs buffered I/O operations for efficiency. However, in scenarios requiring immediate output, such as logging or interactive applications, invoking $stdout.flush forces the buffer to flush, ensuring timely output.

```
Hello, Ruby!
Execution continues after flushing buffer...
```

- **Secure File Paths:** When constructing file paths from user input or external sources, sanitize the input to prevent directory traversal attacks.   Use built-in methods like File.join and File.expand_path to construct safe paths.

```
1  user_input = '../secret/passwords.txt' % Potentially dangerous
2  safe_path = File.join('data', user_input) % Still risky
3  absolute_path = File.expand_path(safe_path, __dir__) % Safer approach
```

- **Use Pathname for Path Manipulations:** The Pathname class provides an object-oriented way to perform path manipulations, making the code cleaner and less error-prone compared to using string manipulations.

```
1  require 'pathname'
2  path = Pathname.new('/usr/local/bin')
3  puts path.dirname % Outputs: "/usr/local"
```

- **Leverage High-level Abstractions:** For I/O actions like serializing and deserializing objects or dealing with web requests, rely on high-level abstractions and libraries such as YAML, JSON, or Net::HTTP to simplify the process and improve maintainability.

```
1  require 'json'
2  data = { name: 'Ruby', version: '3.0' }
3  json_data = data.to_json
4  File.write('version.json', json_data)
```

Incorporating these best practices into Ruby I/O operations enhances the code's resilience, performance, and security, contributing to the development of high-quality applications.

Chapter 10

Working with External Libraries and Gems

This chapter delves into the world of external libraries and gems, a cornerstone of Ruby's extendability and functionality. It guides readers through the process of finding, installing, and managing Ruby gems, the language's packaged libraries. The chapter also introduces Bundler, a tool for managing gem dependencies in Ruby projects, and discusses creating and publishing one's own gems. Additionally, it covers practical aspects of integrating third-party services and APIs using gems. By mastering the use of gems, Ruby developers can leverage existing solutions and contribute to the vibrant ecosystem, enhancing the capability and efficiency of their applications.

10.1 Understanding RubyGems and the Gem Ecosystem

RubyGems, the Ruby community's package manager, serves as the foundational tool for managing Ruby's libraries, known as gems. A

gem is a packaged Ruby application or library that can be easily
shared and installed. The RubyGems ecosystem encompasses not
just the tool itself but also the repository where gems are hosted,
commonly RubyGems.org.

To begin, let's explore how RubyGems facilitates the discovery, installation, and usage of gems. The process starts with the command
gem, which is part of Ruby's standard library. With this command,
users can perform various operations, such as installing, updating,
and listing available gems. For example, installing a gem is as simple as running:

```
1  gem install <gem_name>
```

where <gem_name> is replaced with the name of the gem you wish to
install. This command queries the RubyGems.org repository, finds
the specified gem, downloads it, and installs it on your system.

RubyGems also takes care of managing dependencies between gems.
If the gem you're installing depends on other gems, RubyGems will
automatically resolve and install these dependencies as well. This
feature significantly simplifies the management of complex libraries
that rely on other packages.

Another critical aspect of RubyGems is versioning. Each gem is iden-
tified not just by its name but also by its version number, following
the pattern of major, minor, and patch (e.g., 2.5.1). When you install
a gem, you can specify a particular version:

```
1  gem install <gem_name> -v <version_number>
```

If no version number is specified, RubyGems installs the latest version available. This system allows developers to rely on specific versions of a library, ensuring compatibility and stability within their
projects.

The gem command also supports the listing of all installed gems and
their versions, enabling developers to keep track of their project's
dependencies:

```
1  gem list
```

This command produces an output similar to:

```
*** LOCAL GEMS ***

rails (6.0.3.2)
nokogiri (1.10.10)
puma (4.3.5)
```

Here, we see a list of gems installed locally on the system, along with their versions.

Looking beyond the command-line interface, the RubyGems ecosystem includes the website RubyGems.org, which hosts the repositories of gems. This platform provides an interface for searching and exploring available gems, understanding their documentation, and managing gem versions. Developers can also create and publish their own gems to RubyGems.org, contributing to the community and sharing their work with others.

Understanding the RubyGems ecosystem is crucial for any developer working with Ruby. It not only offers a streamlined way to manage project dependencies but also enables participation in a vibrant community of developers. By leveraging RubyGems, developers can easily incorporate external libraries into their projects, significantly accelerating development and enhancing the functionality of their applications.

10.2 Finding and Selecting Gems for Your Project

Let's delve into the process of finding and selecting gems for your Ruby projects, a task that involves evaluating both the functionality and the quality of the gem. With the RubyGems repository containing thousands of gems, identifying the one that best fits your project requirements is crucial. This section provides a structured approach to streamline the selection process.

Searching for Gems

Begin by searching for gems that potentially meet your project's needs. RubyGems.org, the official Ruby gem hosting service, offers an extensive search functionality. Utilize the following strategies to refine your search:

- Use specific keywords related to the functionality you require. For instance, if you need authentication functionality, keywords could include `"authentication"`, `"OAuth"`, or `"Devise"`.

- Browse through categories and tags that align with your project's domain or functionality needs.

- Review the most downloaded gems or those with a high number of stars, as these indicators often reflect a gem's popularity and community support.

Evaluating Gem Quality

After identifying potential gems, evaluate their quality and suitability for your project by considering the following criteria:

- **Documentation and Examples:** A well-documented gem with clear usage examples significantly lowers the integration time and learning curve.

- **Activity and Maintenance:** Check the gem's repository for recent commits, active maintenance, and responsiveness to issues. An actively maintained gem is less likely to cause issues in the future.

- **Compatibility and Dependencies:** Ensure the gem is compatible with your Ruby and Rails versions. Also, assess its dependencies for potential conflicts with your project.

- **License:** Verify the gem's license to ensure it is compatible with your project's licensing requirements.

244

- **Performance:** Consider the impact of the gem on your project's performance, especially if it is critical. Performance data and benchmarks, if available, can provide valuable insights.

- **Security:** Review any known security vulnerabilities associated with the gem. Sources such as the Ruby Advisory Database offer information on reported security issues.

Testing the Gem

Before fully committing to a gem, it's prudent to test it within your project's environment. This involves:

1. Installing the gem in a development environment, utilizing the gem install command followed by the gem's name.

2. Integrating basic functionality provided by the gem into your application to assess compatibility and performance.

3. Addressing any arising issues or conflicts and determining whether the gem's benefits outweigh these challenges.

Should the initial testing phase reveal insurmountable issues, consider exploring alternative gems that offer similar functionality. Repeating the evaluation and testing process for these alternatives will help in making an informed decision.

Leveraging Community Input

Engage with the Ruby community for insights and feedback on specific gems. Platforms such as Ruby forums, Stack Overflow, and GitHub provide avenues to:

- Ask for recommendations and personal experiences related to the gems you're considering.

- Discuss potential issues or best practices for integrating certain gems into your project.

- Gain insight into how a gem compares to its alternatives in terms of features, performance, and ease of use.

Community input, combined with thorough testing and evaluation, plays a vital role in selecting the right gem for your project, ensuring that you leverage the best available resources to enhance your application's functionality and performance.

10.3   Installing and Managing Gems

Installing and managing Ruby gems is a fundamental skill for Ruby developers, enabling them to enhance the functionality of their applications by leveraging a wide range of external libraries. This section will provide a procedural guide to gem installation, usage, and management, contributing to the efficient development of Ruby applications.

Installing Gems

To install a Ruby gem, the RubyGems package management framework is utilized, which is included with Ruby. The simplest method to install a gem is to use the gem install command followed by the name of the gem. The syntax for this command is as follows:

```
1   gem install [gem_name]
```

For instance, to install the httparty gem, which simplifies making HTTP requests, the following command is used:

```
1   gem install httparty
```

Upon execution, RubyGems will connect to the remote gem repository, defaulting to RubyGems.org, and download the specified gem along with any dependencies it requires. The output of this command will look similar to the following:

```
Successfully installed httparty-0.18.1
1 gem installed
```

Gem Dependencies and Version Management

Gems often depend on other gems. When installing a gem, RubyGems will automatically install all dependencies unless they are already present. To specify a particular version of a gem, the -v flag is used with the version number. For example, to install version 0.17.0 of httparty, the command would be:

```
1  gem install httparty -v 0.17.0
```

For managing different versions of the same gem, RubyGems keeps track of installed versions. It allows specifying the version within a Ruby script using the #gem method. The following line would activate httparty version 0.17.0 in a script:

```
1  gem 'httparty', '0.17.0'
```

Listing and Querying Installed Gems

To inspect which gems are installed, along with their versions, the gem list command is useful. This command outputs a list of installed gems and their respective versions to the console. It can be executed without any parameters as follows:

```
1  gem list
```

To find specific gems or to check if a certain gem is installed, the name of the gem can be passed as a parameter. This action will filter the results. For instance, to find all installed versions of httparty, the command would be:

```
1  gem list httparty
```

Updating Gems

To update installed gems to their latest versions, the gem update command is used. Executing it without any parameters will

247

attempt to update all installed gems. However, to update a specific gem, its name is provided as follows:

```
1   gem update [gem_name]
```

For instance, to update the httparty gem, the command would be:

```
1   gem update httparty
```

Uninstalling Gems

To remove a gem from the system, the gem uninstall command is used, followed by the name of the gem. It is executed as follows:

```
1   gem uninstall [gem_name]
```

For example, to uninstall httparty, the command would be:

```
1   gem uninstall httparty
```

Understanding how to install, manage, and utilize Ruby gems is crucial for developers working with Ruby. By efficiently managing gems and their dependencies, developers can significantly enhance the capability and efficiency of their Ruby applications. With the basics of gem installation and management covered, developers are encouraged to explore more complex aspects of gem management, such as dealing with conflicting dependencies and using Bundler to manage project-specific gemsets.

10.4   Bundler: Defining and Managing Your Project's Dependencies

Bundler is a tool for managing Ruby application's dependencies through a consistent environment for projects by tracking and installing the exact gems and versions that are needed. Essentially, Bundler automates the installation process and ensures that the gems your application depends on are present and up-to-date.

To start using Bundler, you must first install it. If you haven't installed Bundler on your system yet, you can do so by executing the following command in your terminal:

```
gem install bundler
```

Once installed, the next step is to define your project's dependencies within a Gemfile. A Gemfile is a configuration file for Bundler that specifies all of the gems required for your Ruby project. Here is an example of what a Gemfile might look like:

```
source 'https://rubygems.org'

gem 'rails', '6.0.3'
gem 'pg', '~> 0.21'
gem 'puma', '~> 4.1'
gem 'sass-rails', '>= 6'
```

In the Gemfile:

- The source line specifies the rubygems repository that Bundler should use to look for gems.

- Each gem line then declares a dependency required by the project.

- The versioning after the gem name specifies which versions of the gem are acceptable. Bundler will use this to resolve which versions to install.

To install the gems listed in your Gemfile, run:

```
bundle install
```

This command looks at your Gemfile, calculates the best matching versions of each gem (considering all dependencies), installs them on your machine (if they're not already present), and finally generates a Gemfile.lock file.

The Gemfile.lock file captures the exact versions of gems installed, ensuring that all developers working on the project have the same environment:

249

```
GEM
  specs:
    actionpack (6.0.3.4)
    activesupport (6.0.3.4)
    ...

PLATFORMS
  ruby

DEPENDENCIES
  rails (= 6.0.3)
  pg (-> 0.21)
  puma (-> 4.1)
  sass-rails (>= 6)

BUNDLED WITH
   2.2.15
```

If a new developer joins the project or if multiple environments are used, running bundle install using the Gemfile.lock ensures everyone has the same setup. This eradicates the "but it works on my machine" problem.

To update a gem to its newest possible version considering other dependencies, you can run:

```
1   bundle update <gem_name>
```

This updates the gem and its dependencies while also updating the Gemfile.lock file.

Lastly, Bundler can also package all the gems used in your application for offline installation using:

```
1   bundle package
```

This command caches all the gems to vendor/cache within your application, allowing Bundler to install all gems locally without an internet connection using the cached repository.

In summary, Bundler streamlines application development by managing dependencies efficiently, thus enabling developers to focus on programming instead of maintenance. Properly used, Bundler ensures that your project's dependencies are clear, consistent, and easy to manage across different machines and environments.

10.5   Creating Your Own Gem

Creating a Ruby gem is a significant step towards contributing to the Ruby community. This process entails several steps, from structuring the gem to publishing it on RubyGems.org. The following sections will guide you through each step with detailed instructions.

Setting Up Your Gem's Structure

The first step in creating a gem is to set up its basic structure. RubyGems provides a simple command to generate this structure for you.

```
1  gem install bundler
2  bundle gem your_gem_name
```

This command creates a directory named your_gem_name with all the necessary files and directories for your gem. Inside this directory, you will find the gemspec file, which is crucial for defining your gem's properties, such as its name, version, and dependencies.

Editing the Gemspec File

The gemspec file is the heart of your gem. It contains metadata about the gem and a list of files to be included. Open the your_gem_name.gemspec file in your favorite editor and fill in the required information. Below is an example of what this file might look like:

```
1   Gem::Specification.new do |spec|
2     spec.name = "your_gem_name"
3     spec.version = "0.1.0"
4     spec.authors = ["Your Name"]
5     spec.email = ["your.email@example.com"]
6
7     spec.summary = %q{Short summary of your gem}
8     spec.description = %q{Longer description of your gem}
9     spec.homepage = "http://example.com/your_gem_name"
10    spec.license = "MIT"
11
```

```
12  spec.files = Dir["lib/**/*.rb", "bin/*", "README.md"]
13  spec.bindir = "bin"
14  spec.executables = spec.files.grep(%r{\Abin/}) { |f| File.basename(f) }
15  spec.require_paths = ["lib"]
16
17  spec.add_dependency "some_dependency", "~> 1.0"
18
19  spec.add_development_dependency "rake", "~> 10.0"
20  end
```

Make sure to replace the placeholder values with actual information about your gem.

Writing Your Code

With the gem structure and gemspec file in place, you can start writing your gem's code. Code for your gem should be placed in the lib/your_gem_name directory. For example, if your gem is named "awesome_gem", your main module file should be named lib/awesome_gem.rb.

```
1  module AwesomeGem
2    def self.hello
3      puts "Hello from AwesomeGem!"
4    end
5  end
```

Building Your Gem

Once you have written your gem's code, it's time to build it. Building your gem packages it into a .gem file, which can be distributed and installed.

```
1  gem build your_gem_name.gemspec
```

This command generates a .gem file named after your gem with a version number, for example, your_gem_name-0.1.0.gem.

Publishing Your Gem

After building your gem, you can publish it to RubyGems.org, making it available for installation by the Ruby community.

First, you need to create an account on RubyGems.org if you don't already have one. Next, use the following command to push your gem to RubyGems.org:

```
1  gem push your_gem_name-0.1.0.gem
```

You will be prompted to enter your RubyGems.org credentials. Once authenticated, your gem will be uploaded and available for anyone to install using gem `install your_gem_name`.

Managing Your Gem

After publishing your gem, it is important to manage it by addressing user issues, updating it with new features, and fixing bugs. This may involve releasing new versions of the gem. Remember to update the version number in your `.gemspec` file and rebuild the gem each time you release a new version.

Creating and maintaining a Ruby gem can be a rewarding experience. It not only contributes to the Ruby ecosystem but also allows developers worldwide to benefit from your work. Follow these steps, and you will be well on your way to becoming a Ruby gem author.

10.6 Publishing Your Gem to RubyGems.org

Publishing your gem to RubyGems.org is a significant step towards contributing to the Ruby community. This process allows your gem to be easily accessible and utilized by developers worldwide. Before initiating the publication process, ensure that your gem adheres to the naming conventions established by RubyGems.org to avoid conflicts and confusion. Additionally, it is vital to include comprehensive documentation and specify dependency versions accurately to facilitate a seamless integration for users.

Preparation Before Publishing

Before publishing your gem, several preparatory steps are necessary:

- Review your gem's naming to ensure it is unique and descriptive.

- Update the .gemspec file with accurate information about the gem, including authors, email, summary, and description.

- Document your APIs thoroughly. Utilize tools like YARD to generate professional documentation.

- Ensure that your gemspec declares all dependencies with appropriate version constraints to prevent conflicts.

- Run your test suite and ensure all tests pass to confirm the gem's stability.

Building Your Gem

To package your gem, use the gem build command followed by your gemspec file. This action creates a .gem file that encapsulates your library.

```
1   gem build your_gem_name.gemspec
```

Creating an Account on RubyGems.org

If you do not already have an account on RubyGems.org, you will need to create one. Visit the RubyGems.org website and follow the registration process. You will need to verify your email address to activate your account.

Publishing the Gem

With your .gem file prepared and your account set up, you are ready to publish. Use the gem push command to upload your gem to RubyGems.org.

```
1  gem push your_gem_name-version.gem
```

Upon successful upload, RubyGems.org will process your gem, making it available for installation via the gem install command.

Post-Publication

After publishing your gem, consider the following best practices to maintain and promote your gem:

- Regularly update your gem to fix bugs, add features, and update dependencies.

- Monitor feedback from users and address issues promptly.

- Promote your gem through social media, blog posts, and Ruby conferences or meetups.

Publishing a gem to RubyGems.org is more than just a technical process; it is a contribution to the Ruby ecosystem. By following the steps outlined above, you can ensure that your gem is accessible, usable, and benefits the broader Ruby community.

10.7 External APIs: Working with Web Services

Working with external Application Programming Interfaces (APIs) significantly enhances the capabilities of Ruby applications by interfacing with web services. This section describes the process of consuming external APIs using Ruby gems, specifically focusing on the `httparty` and `faraday` gems. These tools simplify the task of sending HTTP requests and parsing responses. The procedure elaborated here includes identifying the API, configuring the gem, crafting the request, and handling the response.

To initiate, one must install the required gem. For demonstration purposes, the `httparty` gem will be used. Installation is conducted through the RubyGems package manager as shown below:

```
1  gem install httparty
```

Upon successful installation of the `httparty` gem, it's necessary to require it in your Ruby script to utilize its features.

```
1  require 'httparty'
```

Subsequently, identifying the endpoint of the external API you intend to interact with is crucial. As an example, we'll use a fictitious API providing weather data: `https://api.weather.com/v1/forecast`. The subsequent step involves crafting your request. With the `httparty` gem, making a GET request to the API can be achieved as follows:

```
1  response = HTTParty.get('https://api.weather.com/v1/forecast?city=London&units=
        metric')
```

In this request, two query parameters are passed: `city` and `units`, specifying the city for which weather data is sought and the unit of measurement, respectively.

Once the request is made, handling the response is paramount. The response from the API can be checked for success and parsed to extract necessary information.

```
1  if response.success?
2    weather_data = response.parsed_response
3  else
4    puts "Failed to retrieve data"
5  end
```

`response.success?` checks whether the request was successful, and `response.parsed_response` parses the JSON response into a Ruby hash, making it easy to navigate and use the data.

For enhanced functionality, such as setting headers or authenticating API requests, the `httparty` gem offers comprehensive options. For example, to add headers to the request, one can modify the GET request as follows:

```
1  response = HTTParty.get('https://api.weather.com/v1/forecast?city=London&units=
       metric',
2                          headers: { "Authorization" => "Bearer YOUR_API_KEY" })
```

The `headers` option allows for the inclusion of necessary headers, in this case, an authorization header crucial for accessing secured APIs.

In summary, leveraging external APIs in Ruby applications through gems like `httparty` involves installation of the gem, requiring it in your script, crafting the request with appropriate parameters and options, and effectively handling the response. This approach not only augments the functionality of Ruby applications but also integrates a wealth of services and data available via external APIs.

10.8   Using ActiveRecord Outside of Rails

ActiveRecord, Rails' default Object-Relational Mapping (ORM) system, is renowned for its ease of use in managing database interactions within Rails applications. However, its utility extends beyond the Rails ecosystem, providing a powerful tool for database manipulation in standalone Ruby applications. This section will discuss how to leverage ActiveRecord outside of Rails, enabling Ruby developers to utilize its ORM capabilities in any Ruby project.

First, to use ActiveRecord in a non-Rails application, it must be included in your project's Gemfile. The following line should be added:

```
1  gem 'activerecord', '~> 6.0'
```

After adding ActiveRecord to your Gemfile, run `bundle install` to install the gem and its dependencies.

Next, establish a connection to your database. ActiveRecord supports multiple database systems such as SQLite, PostgreSQL, and MySQL. For a SQLite database, the connection can be established as follows:

```
1  require 'active_record'
2
3  ActiveRecord::Base.establish_connection(
4    adapter: 'sqlite3',
5    database: 'your_database_name_here.sqlite3'
6  )
```

The establish_connection method initializes the database connection using the specified configuration. Replace 'your_database_name_here.sqlite3' with the path to your SQLite database file.

With the database connection set up, you can define models that inherit from ActiveRecord::Base. This empowers them with ActiveRecord's ORM capabilities. Here is an example of a simple model called User:

```
1  class User < ActiveRecord::Base
2  end
```

This User model automatically maps to the users table in the database, assuming ActiveRecord's naming conventions are followed. The model provides methods to perform standard CRUD (Create, Read, Update, Delete) operations and query the database.

To create a new user, you can use:

```
1  user = User.create(name: 'John Doe', email: 'johndoe@example.com')
```

To query the database for users, ActiveRecord offers a variety of methods, such as:

```
1  all_users = User.all
2  first_user = User.first
3  user = User.find_by(name: 'John Doe')
```

Performing complex queries and utilizing associations (such as has_many, belongs_to) is also possible with ActiveRecord outside of Rails, following the same syntax and method calls as within a Rails application.

For handling migrations in a non-Rails project, ActiveRecord provides the `ActiveRecord::Migrator` class. Migrations can be defined in pure Ruby using ActiveRecord's DSL, and then executed to modify the database schema:

```
ActiveRecord::Migration.create_table :users do |t|
  t.string :name
  t.string :email

  t.timestamps
end
```

Using ActiveRecord outside of Rails requires setting up the gem, establishing a database connection, and then leveraging ActiveRecord's models and migrations just as you would in a Rails application. This approach allows Ruby developers to utilize a robust ORM tool in standalone projects, benefiting from ActiveRecord's features and syntactic conveniences without the overhead of a full Rails stack.

10.9 Security Considerations When Using Gems

[This section is intentionally left blank for continuity]

10.10 Troubleshooting Common Issues with Gems

[This section is intentionally left blank for continuity]

10.11   Integrating Third-Party Services with Gems

Given the importance of including third-party services in modern Ruby applications, this section explores how gems facilitate such integration smoothly and efficiently. These external services can range from payment processing systems, email providers, to social media APIs. Utilizing gems for this purpose not only expedites development but also ensures that Ruby applications are scalable, maintainable, and feature-rich.

Selecting the Right Gem

The first step in integrating a third-party service is to select an appropriate gem that acts as a wrapper for the service's API. This typically involves:

- Researching available gems on RubyGems.org or GitHub to find those dedicated to the service of interest.

- Evaluating the gem's popularity, maintenance status, and compatibility with your Ruby version to ensure reliability.

- Reading through documentation and existing code examples to understand the gem's usability and functionality.

Installation and Configuration

Upon selecting a suitable gem, it should be added to your application's Gemfile:

```
1  gem 'some_third_party_service_gem', '~> 1.0'
```

Running the $ bundle install command will install the gem and its dependencies. Configuration usually involves initializing the gem with your application-specific credentials, which may involve creating an initializer file under the `config/initializers` directory:

```
SomeThirdPartyServiceGem.configure do |config|
    config.api_key = 'YOUR_API_KEY'
    config.other_configuration = 'Other required configuration'
end
```

Using the Gem to Connect to the Third-Party Service

Integrating the third-party service into your application typically involves calling the gem's methods to perform operations provided by the service. For example, to send an email using an email service provider gem:

```
mail = SomeEmailServiceGem::Email.new do
    from 'no-reply@yourdomain.com'
    to 'user@example.com'
    subject 'Welcome to Our Service'
    body 'Your account has been successfully created.'
end
mail.deliver
```

Error Handling

When integrating third-party services, handling errors gracefully is crucial. Many gems offer built-in mechanisms for error handling which should be leveraged to ensure your application remains robust and reliable. A basic implementation may look like:

```
begin
    # Attempt to execute a service operation
    response = SomeThirdPartyServiceGem.operation(arguments)
rescue SomeThirdPartyServiceGem::Error => e
    # Handle error, possibly logging it or notifying administrators
    puts "An error occurred: #{e.message}"
end
```

Best Practices

Finally, some best practices when using gems to integrate third-party services include:

- Regularly updating the gem to receive the latest bug fixes and features.

- Reviewing the gem's source and contributions if it's open-source, to ensure it follows secure coding practices.

- Monitor and potentially limit the number of API calls in accordance with the service's rate limits.

- Encrypt sensitive information like API keys and tokens, preferably using environment variables.

As detailed in this section, integrating third-party services using gems is a streamlined process that enhances Ruby applications' functionality significantly. By carefully selecting, installing, and using these gems following the best practices outlined, developers can efficiently leverage external services while maintaining application security and performance.

10.12   Security Considerations When Using Gems

When incorporating external libraries or gems into a Ruby application, it is paramount to consider the security implications. External dependencies can introduce vulnerabilities, potentially compromising the security of the application. This section outlines key practices to mitigate security risks when using gems.

- **Vet Gems Before Inclusion:** Before adding a new gem to the project, conduct a thorough analysis. Assess the gem's source, its community reputation, the frequency of updates, and its compatibility with the project's existing infrastructure. Tools such as RubyGems.org provide valuable insights into a gem's version history, download statistics, and documentation, serving as indicators of its reliability and security stance.

- **Use Automated Vulnerability Scanners:** Leverage tools such as Bundler-audit or Ruby Advisory Database to automatically scan your project's Gemfile for known vulnerabilities. These tools compare the versions of gems specified in your project against a database of known security flaws. For example, to scan your project with Bundler-audit, you would run the following command:

```
1  bundle exec bundler-audit check --update
```

The `--update` flag ensures that the database of known vulnerabilities is up to date before scanning.

- **Employ Continuous Integration (CI) Security Checks:** Integrate security checks into your CI pipeline. Tools like GitHub Actions or GitLab CI can automate the execution of vulnerability scans every time code is pushed to the repository. This practice helps in early identification and resolution of security issues.

- **Adopt Semantic Versioning Practices:** When specifying gem versions in the Gemfile, use semantic versioning principles to balance between stability and receiving security updates. For instance, specifying a gem dependency as follows limits updates to only patch-level changes, reducing the risk of introducing breaking changes while staying updated with security patches.

```
1  gem 'nokogiri', '~> 1.10.4'
```

- **Monitor Dependencies Regularly:** Even after a gem has been vetted and added to a project, it's crucial to continuously monitor it for new vulnerabilities. Dependency management tools like Dependabot can automatically create pull requests to update gems when new versions are released, facilitating timely application of security patches.

- **Review Third-Party Code:** While it may not always be feasible to conduct a line-by-line code review for every gem, scrutinizing the source code of critical dependencies can reveal potential security concerns that automated tools might miss. Pay particular attention to gems that deal with authentication, encryption, or network communications.

- **Limit Gem Installation Sources:** Restrict the sources from which gems can be installed to trusted repositories. By default, Bundler fetches gems from RubyGems.org, but additional sources can be specified. It is advisable to avoid adding unknown or untrusted sources to the Gemfile or gemspec files. To specify RubyGems.org as the source, use the following syntax:

```
1   source 'https://rubygems.org'
```

- **Handle API Keys and Sensitive Data Carefully:** Avoid hardcoding secrets or API keys directly in the source code. Instead, use environment variables or encrypted secrets management tools to handle sensitive information. This approach reduces the risk of exposing credentials in the event of a security breach.

While gems significantly enhance the functionality and efficiency of Ruby applications, they also introduce potential security risks. Adhering to the practices outlined in this section can mitigate these risks, enabling developers to leverage the power of the Ruby ecosystem with confidence.

10.13   Troubleshooting Common Issues with Gems

Handling gem-related issues efficiently is essential for keeping a Ruby project operational. This section will discuss various common problems developers might encounter while working with gems and provide strategies for resolution.

1. Gem Installation Failures

A common problem faced when managing gems is the failure of gem installation. This can occur due to network issues, permissions problems, or version conflicts.

- To resolve network issues, ensure that your internet connection is stable and that your firewall or proxy settings do not block RubyGems requests. If you're behind a corporate proxy, configure gem to use the proxy by setting the HTTP_PROXY environment variable.

- If the issue is related to permissions, running the gem installation command with sudo may resolve the problem. However, using sudo to install gems is generally discouraged because it can lead to security vulnerabilities and mess with version management. Instead, it's advisable to manage gems with a version manager like RVM or rbenv that installs gems in the user's home directory.

- For version conflicts, ensure that the gem's dependencies do not conflict with the versions of already installed gems. You can specify version requirements directly in the Gemfile to avoid such conflicts.

2. Bundler Could Not Find Compatible Versions for a Gem

This error occurs when Bundler cannot resolve the dependency tree due to incompatible gem versions. The output typically includes which gem versions are in conflict.

```
1  Bundler could not find compatible versions for gem "rails":
2    In Gemfile:
3      rails (= 5.1.0)
4
5      my_custom_gem (-> 0.2.0) was resolved to 0.2.0, which depends on
6        rails (-> 5.2.0)
```

To resolve this, you may need to update the version constraint of the conflicting gem in the Gemfile. Alternatively, running bundle update <gem_name> updates the gem to a newer version that may resolve the conflict.

3. Gems Not Found in Production

Occasionally, a gem working perfectly in development might not be found in the production environment. This usually occurs due to discrepancies in how gems are being managed across environments.

- Ensure that all required gems are listed in your Gemfile, not just installed locally via gem install. Also, make sure the Gemfile.lock file is checked into version control to keep a consistent set of gems across all environments.

- Verify that the environment variables set in production match those expected by the application, particularly those related to Gem paths.

4. LoadError: Cannot Load Such File – SomeGem

This error signifies that Ruby is unable to load a specified gem, highlighting either installation issues or problems in the way Ruby is configured to find gems.

```
LoadError: cannot load such file -- some_gem
```

To troubleshoot, confirm that the gem is installed by running gem list. If the gem is missing, install it using gem install some_gem. If the gem is present but still not found, inspect the $LOAD_PATH to ensure it includes the directories where RubyGems installs gems. This can be done by running echo $LOAD_PATH in your terminal.

5. Native Extension Build Failures

Some gems come with native extensions, C or C++ code that needs to be compiled on the host system. Compilation failures can occur duc to missing development tools or headers.

- On MacOS, ensure that Xcode Command Line Tools are installed. This can be done by running xcode-select --install.

- On Ubuntu or Debian-based systems, installing the build-essential package provides the necessary compilation tools. Use the command sudo apt-get install build-essential.

266

- Ensure that all required libraries for the gem's extensions are installed. Check the gem's documentation for any additional dependency requirements.

Troubleshooting gem issues involves diagnosing and addressing network problems, permissions errors, version conflicts, and environment discrepancies. Applying the mentioned solutions effectively can resolve most problems encountered while working with gems, leading to a smoother development workflow.

10.14 Keeping Your Gems Updated

Keeping your gems updated is vital for ensuring the security, performance, and compatibility of your Ruby applications. With the rapid evolution of software, vulnerabilities are regularly discovered in older versions of gems, and new features are introduced in the updates. Inadequately maintained gem dependencies can introduce operational risks to applications. This section outlines methods to effectively manage and update your Ruby gems.

Understanding Versioning in Gems: Before delving into updating gems, it's crucial to understand semantic versioning (SemVer) used by most gems. Semantic versioning is structured as MAJOR.MINOR.PATCH, where:

- MAJOR versions introduce incompatible API changes,

- MINOR versions add functionality in a backwards-compatible manner,

- PATCH versions include backwards-compatible bug fixes.

Understanding the versioning scheme aids in assessing the impact of updating a particular gem on your project.

Using `bundle outdated` to Identify Outdated Gems: To check for gems in need of updates within a project, use the `bundle outdated` command. This command lists all gems that have newer versions available than those specified in the Gemfile.lock. Consider this command as a starting point for updating your gems.

Updating Gems with `bundle update`**:** To update a specific gem, use the command `bundle update ⟨gem_name⟩`. This command will try to update the specified gem and its dependencies while respecting the version constraints defined in your Gemfile. For updating all gems, simply running `bundle update` without specifying a gem name will attempt to update all dependencies to their latest versions that still satisfy the Gemfile constraints.

Handling Major Version Updates Carefully: When updating to a new major version of a gem, it is advisable to review the gem's changelog and upgrade guide, if available. Major version updates can introduce changes that are not backwards compatible, requiring modifications in your application code. Testing is essential after such updates to ensure that your application continues to function correctly.

Automating Gem Updates: Several tools can automate the process of keeping gems updated. Dependabot, for example, is a service integrated into GitHub that monitors your repository's Gemfile for outdated gems and automatically creates pull requests to update them. Using such tools can reduce the manual overhead of keeping gems updated and help in maintaining the security and health of your Ruby applications.

Security Updates: Prioritize the update of gems with known security vulnerabilities. Services like Ruby Advisory Database provide information about gems with security issues. It's crucial to update these gems immediately to protect your application from potential exploits.

Testing After Updates: Regardless of the method used to update gems, thorough testing is imperative to ensure that the updates do not introduce regression or break functionality. Automated test suites and continuous integration (CI) pipelines play a pivotal role in validating the updates' compatibility with your application.

Maintaining an up-to-date gem environment is a continuous responsibility that, when managed properly, significantly contributes to the robustness and security of Ruby applications. Leveraging tools like Bundler, Dependabot, and adhering to best practices in gem versioning and testing can streamline the process of keeping gems updated while minimizing the risk of introducing issues into your application.

www.ingramcontent.com/pod-product-compliance
Lightning Source LLC
LaVergne TN
LVHW022338060326
832902LV00022B/4114